In Spirit and I

Devotional Thoughts and Praye

Marty Parks

Lorenz

Lorenz Publishing Company
P.O. Box 802
Dayton OH 45401-0802

Editor: Julie Eisenhauer
Book Design: WordStreamCopy
Cover Design: Patti Jeffers

Lorenz Publishing Company
A division of The Lorenz Corporation
P.O. Box 802
Dayton, OH 45401-0802
www.lorenz.com

Printed in the United States of America

ISBN: 978-0-7877-5744-1

2

Contents

4

Foreword

Several years ago, the choir in my church undertook a four-week study to identify some significant scripture passages that would serve as a biblical foundation for our ministry. From those, we selected four to serve as the main "pillars" that would guide us and give us focus. It was incredibly insightful and wonderfully rewarding to dig into the Word and discover for ourselves what God had to say about worship and about those who lead it. We ended up with a fresh sense of our calling and a renewed passion to fulfill it.

And that's what led to this volume you're looking at right now! Here are sixty devotional thoughts, based on sixty significant scripture passages, that are designed to encourage you and prompt you, whether you're a worship leader, a worship ministry participant, or anyone "following hard after God." For all of us, worship itself is a response—a response to God for all He is and for all He's done. You'll read a lot about that concept in these pages.

You might choose this book as a companion to your own personal devotional times. Each entry includes a pertinent scripture passage along with a key verse. A few minutes each day to quietly let God's Word wash over you may be just what you need.

Or it could be that a group study is more in line for you right now. Walking through these thoughts alongside those with whom you serve could be a rich and unifying experience, allowing everyone to be, literally, "on the same page." The questions at the end of each entry were designed for that very thing. I hope they prompt some thoughtful discussion.

God has said that His Word would not return to Him void. My prayer for you is that as you allow His Word to dwell in you richly, you'll see again—or maybe for the very first time—that the worship of God is the highest calling of the believer.

Marty Parks

1
God-Breathed

✦ 2 Timothy 3:14–17 ✦

All Scripture is God-breathed and is useful for teaching,
rebuking, correcting and training in righteousness.
(2 Timothy 3:16)

The validity of any worship ministry is best judged by its adherence to the Word of God. Styles come and go; trends appear then fade; personal preferences are, well, personal and individual; and traditions vary from one congregation to the next. In the end, none of these determine the ultimate impact of our ministries. Only a fundamental basis and application derived from scripture will suffice.

And that's a really good place to start as we begin looking at significant scripture passages that will help us create and sustain an effective and God-honoring worship ministry. Today's key verse, verse 16, mentions the phrase "God-breathed," or as it says in some translations, "inspired by God." The Greek word used here is *theopneustos*, and it literally means "God-breathed," or "due to the inspiration of God." Many believe that the apostle Paul may well have coined this term, and the overall sense of the verse is that each and every individual scripture is sacred and profitable for teaching, training, and correction.

You see, the messages we convey are important and the words we employ are vital. The musical components of our worship will have lasting effect, and while we all strive for excellence—which does indeed honor God—those we serve will be affected much longer and more deeply by the truths of God's Word than by the perfection of our performance.

O God, may Your Word be the guiding principle
in our worship as we seek to convey Your
greatness and Your grace. Keep us grounded
in Your truth. Amen

- How closely does the worship ministry you're involved with adhere to the Word of God?
- What steps can you take to ensure that this ministry is properly grounded?

Notes...

2
In Spirit and in Truth

"Yet a time is coming and has now come when the true worshipers will worship the Father in spirit and in truth, for they are the kind of worshipers the Father seeks."
(John 4:23)

I love this story for a lot of reasons, not the least of which is the sheer boldness of the woman Jesus encounters. For starters, she has three strikes against her at the outset of this dialog. She's a woman—a second-class citizen in the view of many in the culture of that day. Then, she's a Samaritan—worse than a second-class citizen. No self-respecting Jewish man would be caught dead speaking with someone of that lineage. Finally, she's been married more than a couple of times, and the guy she's living with now hasn't even tied the knot with her.

Jesus apparently knows all about her, and she perceives Him as a prophet. Immediately she turns the discussion to one about worship, specifically, one about stylistic differences and preferences. This is sort of a precursor to our discussions today over the unfortunately-labeled *worship wars*. "Our fathers worshiped on this mountain," she says, "but you Jews worship in Jerusalem" (John 4:20). (Sound familiar? *We say stained glass, hymnals, and a pipe organ; but you say theatre lighting, projected lyrics, and a band.*)

Jesus cuts her off at the pass and enlightens her to the fact that worship isn't about location, atmosphere, accompaniment, or architecture. It's not even about style. It *is*, however, about spirit and truth. It *is* about a passionate offering of ourselves to the God who had revealed Himself to us in His Son. And it's all about the God we seek desperately to know.

A pastor friend of mine says that worship without spirit is dead orthodoxy. And worship without truth is shallow emotionalism. You have to have both.

Ultimately, what the Father seeks is really none of the things we get hung up about. He's not seeking personalities or programs or song sets. He's seeking *worshipers*.

That's me and that's you.

- What externals cause distraction or division in your worship life?
- What steps can you take to ensure that what's really important is what's really focused on?

Notes…

3
As with One Voice

❖ 2 Chronicles 5:11–14 ❖

The trumpeters and singers joined in unison, as with one voice, to give praise and thanks to the LORD.
(2 Chronicles 5:13a)

You remember the story. Israel's temple, for the worship of God, had *finally* been constructed. Under King Solomon's direction, what had been a passion for his father, David, was now a reality. The final step in the ceremonial liturgy was the entrance of the Ark of the Covenant into the temple itself. You might recall that for generations the Ark represented to the people the very presence of God Himself. So, this was a pretty big deal!

Can you see it? All the priests who are musicians are lined up on the east side of the altar, splendidly-arrayed and well-rehearsed. And they're accompanied by 120 other priests playing trumpets. (Talk about your balance problem!) The singers and instrumentalists combine to offer a glorious anthem—"He is good; his love endures forever!" And suddenly God's presence is manifest in the form of a cloud so thick that the priests can't perform their service. The glory of God has totally and unmistakably filled the temple!

Now, this is important—read it slowly. It wasn't the number of musicians or the hours of preparation that prompted the revealing of God's presence. I'm convinced that the key is found in verse 13 of today's reading: "The trumpeters and singers joined in unison, *as with one voice…*"

Rehearsal and logistical preparation are vital ingredients when it comes to leading worship. I really believe God honors these sorts of things, and I think we'd all agree that how we approach the act of worship speaks volumes concerning how we feel about the One being worshiped. But without unity, we're left with, well, just a lot of rehearsal and logistical preparation.

So, go back and read that story one more time. I'm sure you'll see it—a unified, whole-hearted devotion to the worship of God. It wasn't a matter of style, or of instrumentation, or the number of participants, or any petty differences they might have had.

It was a matter of the heart.

10

*O God, may our personal and corporate worship reflect a unity of spirit
and a whole-hearted desire to honor only You. Reveal to us the glory of
Your presence; we pray in Jesus' name. Amen*

- What distractions or hindrances cause you to miss seeing the glory of God?
- How can you overcome or eliminate these?

Notes...

4
How Big is Your Worship Team?

❖ 1 Chronicles 15:16–22 ❖

Kenaniah the head Levite was in charge of the singing;
that was his responsibility because he was skillful at it.
(1 Chronicles 15:22)

Just to set the scene: the city of Jerusalem had been built up by King David, and its crowning glory was to be the return of the Ark of the Covenant—that visible, tangible reminder of God's presence among His people. While David appointed the Levites to appoint others in all sorts of worship leadership roles, it appears that careful attention was given to making assignments according to particular gifts, skills, and abilities. That's why Kenaniah, the head Levite, was in charge of the singing—he was good at it!

All of us in the Body of Christ have been gifted in some way, and your worship team is probably bigger than you think. It's not just the choir, or praise team, or instrumentalists, or any of the other "up front" people that are visible on stage. It's also the tech crew (however simple or complex their job may be), the ushers and greeters, and even the grounds crew and those who maintain your facility. Here's why: everything that people encounter once they step onto your church property on Sunday morning affects their worship experience. And everyone responsible for, or involved in, what these people encounter is part of your worship team. Utilizing their gifts and their passions, they're worship leaders all right. The only question is: what kind will they be?

Oh, and by the way, do you remember a guy named Bezalel? The opening of Exodus 31 gives us a hint at his background. He was a craftsman, a builder, put in charge of the construction of the Tent of Meeting (the tabernacle) because of his "skill, ability and knowledge," another confirmation of a gifted person released to exercise his gift. A blue-collar construction-worker kind of guy doing his thing to the glory of God.

But get this: Bezalel is the very first person mentioned in scripture said to be *filled with the Spirit of God.*

Father, give us the courage to use our gifts for Your glory
and our abilities for Your praise. In all we do, may the
work of our hands point to the greatness of our God. Amen

- How effectively are people in your congregation being utilized according to their gifts, abilities, and passions?
- How big is your worship team?

5
Equipping the Saints

"That will make your load lighter, because they will share it with you."
(Exodus 18:22b)

"What you are doing is not good!" Under normal circumstances, none of us wants to hear those words. But that's exactly what Moses' father-in-law, Jethro, said to him in regard to Moses attempting to hear and judge every single case that came before him during the Israelites' desert journey. In essence, Jethro was telling him, "Spread out all this work and recruit some assistants. Get some help!"

That's pretty good advice for those of us involved in worship ministry, whether in a leadership role or in a position of supportive involvement. When we distribute responsibilities, we accomplish greater things. When we decentralize our ministry, we help everyone "buy into" it. Everybody feels ownership, and everybody has an investment in something greater than they are. In short, we can accomplish more together than we ever could individually.

I think that's at least a part of what the apostle Paul had in mind when he wrote,

> *It was he who gave some to be apostles, some to be prophets, some to be evangelists, and some to be pastors and teachers, to prepare God's people for works of service, so that the body of Christ may be built up until we all reach unity in the faith and in the knowledge of the Son of God and become mature, attaining to the whole measure of the fullness of Christ. (Ephesians 4:11–13)*

After all, if you're a worship leader, or in a leadership role of any kind in the church, your task is not to do all the work. Your task is to equip the saints.

Lord Jesus, Your gifting to Your people is amazing. Help us to recognize, to receive, and to respond to what You've given us. Amen

- What roles are you currently filling that might be better handled by someone else?
- Who do you know that would be perfect for some ministry role in your church?

Notes...

6
A Word about the Word

✦ Colossians 3:15–16 ✦

Let the word of Christ dwell in you richly as you teach
and admonish one another with all wisdom, and as you
sing psalms, hymns and spiritual songs with gratitude
in your hearts to God.
(Colossians 3:16)

Variety in the Body of Christ and variety in the worship of God is a good and healthy thing. Different viewpoints, different histories, different traditions, different responses—the God we worship is far too great and far too multi-faceted to be approached, honored, and worshiped by any one system or style.

For the longest time, I relied on today's key verse, Colossians 3:16, as a justification—a defense, maybe—for incorporating a variety of musical styles in worship. I think that's probably a valid precedent. Greek scholars would tell us that "psalms" indicates pretty much what we'd think it does—artistic creations directed to God or in praise of God like anthems or other "presentational" music. "Hymns" seem to have been, even in the first century, well-known and accepted congregational expressions of praise or testimony. (By the way, Philippians 2:6–11 is most likely one of the earliest hymns of the Church. That's why it's probably indented in your Bible.) And then we see "spiritual songs," which appear to be newly composed, fresh, and more intimate offerings to God. That brings to mind modern worship songs, doesn't it?

But I'm convinced that the real issue doesn't lie in the diversity of musical styles we incorporate (how old or how new; how updated or how traditional). The real issue—the key to it all, really—is contained in that very first phrase: "Let the word of Christ dwell in you richly…"

Without that, our gatherings are just a hodge-podge of influences, expressions, styles, and preferences. But with that, we're united by what really counts.

Jesus, Your Word is a lamp to our feet and a light to our path. May
our worship reflect Your radiance as Your Word dwells richly in us. Amen

- How present is scripture, the Word of Christ, in the gatherings of your worship community?
- In what ways can you further incorporate or highlight scripture?

Notes...

7
In Touch to Receive

❖ Proverbs 29:18–20 ❖

Where there is no revelation, the people cast off restraint;
but blessed is he who keeps the law.
(Proverbs 29:18)

We must be in touch *with* God to receive the vital word *from* God. That's a concept worth investing in, and as we know, investments can cost us something. But in the best of cases, they're so worth it.

Chances are that, somewhere along the way, you've been involved with a church that's undertaken some sort of building campaign. Maybe it was a project to construct new educational space, a new kitchen, or maybe a new sanctuary or worship center. And if your experience is like mine, somewhere along the way, the words from Proverbs 29:18 were referenced: "Where there is no vision, the people perish" (KJV). Rather than thinking of this as "If we don't have a good idea or concept (vision), our efforts will be useless; we're going to die on the vine," I discovered a few things that have really solidified this verse as a foundational one for our worship ministries.

The word we normally see translated as "vision" is the Hebrew word *chazown*, and it means "revelation, oracle, or word from God." It's the same word we see in 1 Samuel 3:1, where we read, "In those days the word of the LORD was rare; there were not many visions." Secondly, the word *para* is used in regard to "the people." *Para* indicates "unprotected or unrestrained; going one's own way." You could interpret this verse to say, "Where there is no oracle, no word from God, the people are unrestrained and unprotected."

Far too many times, we've seen ministries that were built on personalities, programs, traditions, styles, architecture, or whatever. They're ministries built not on the Word of God, but on the efforts of men. As you know (and, unfortunately, may have experienced) that can lead to catastrophe! Singing, sharing, and really diving into the Word of God, personally and with the members of your worship team, are crucial. Otherwise, we're just sort of doing our own thing, left to our own devices.

Again, we must be in touch *with* God to receive the vital word *from* God.

- What steps can you take to ensure that God's Word is a vital part of your worship ministry?
- How can you personally be in closer touch with God?

Notes...

8
An Unbelievable Assertion

❀ Hebrews 10:19–25 ❀

And let us consider how we may spur one another on toward
love and good deeds.
(Hebrews 10:24)

Go back and read today's scripture passage again. No, really. Go back and read it again; only this time, imagine that you're a first-century Jewish convert to faith in Christ. For you, Judaism has been your religion, your culture, your nationality, your ethnicity…your everything.

Most likely, you would have heard this letter (the book of Hebrews) in a house church meeting. The images mentioned in this passage would have immediately drawn your mind to the customs and rituals of the tabernacle and the temple—priests entering the Most Holy Place after ceremonial washing and the sprinkling of the blood of a sacrificial animal. But get this: the writer of this letter is suggesting to the early Church, and to us, that *we* have access to the Most Holy Place (where God met, and still meets, with His people); the curtain separating God and man has been torn in two. *We* have *our* hearts sprinkled with the blood of the ultimate Sacrifice. *We* have not only our hands washed (as the ancient priests did), but also our entire bodies.

We have access to God. An incredible, unbelievable assertion on the part of this writer! And what it means for us is this: the old has become new; everything that those early believers had witnessed for generations has given way to a brand new idea; and what was once symbolic is now reality.

This could change everything, you know. We really should think about our approach to and interaction with God, and with each other: not neglecting the priority of worship, but spurring each other on, encouraging each other when we're together, and sharing stories of how God has worked in our lives and can work in theirs. Supporting, spurring, encouraging.

By the way, it's really hard to tear somebody down when you're building them up.

Father, thank You for allowing us access to You through the sacrifice
of Jesus. Give us the courage to encourage. Amen

- Is there something in your worship of God that you sense He wants to begin altering?
- How would an understanding of "access to God" change the concept of worship in your church?

Notes...

9
A Transformed Reality

◈ John 2:1–11 ◈

This, the first of his miraculous signs, Jesus performed in
Cana in Galilee. He thus revealed his glory, and his disciples
put their faith in him.
(John 2:11)

"I just didn't get anything out of that worship service!"

Ever heard that? Ever said it yourself? One thing I've discovered is that what I, personally, receive in a worship experience depends heavily and directly on what I, personally, put in. My preparation before and my attitude as I approach are often the most important factors in determining how I'll respond in a worship setting. After all, we're not called to receive; we're called to give. Whatever we receive is just the fortunate by-product of responding to God in worship.

Have you ever wondered why Jesus would choose as His first miracle (at least, His first publicly recorded miracle) something so trivial, so "worldly" as turning water into wine? Why in the world wouldn't He have burst onto the scene, dazzling us with some death-defying resurrection, a gravity-ignoring lake-top stroll, or at the very least, a healing? It makes you wonder why He would go with this hedonistic, appeals-to-the-flesh kind of demonstration.

Could it be that God was saying again that something new is about to occur? That we're about to see Him in ways we never could have imagined? Maybe the whole point is this: *Just as the water jars, used for purification rites or ceremonial cleansing, were to be filled with something fresh, our worship rituals are to be emptied and replaced with a brand new filling of Him.*

We could all probably ask ourselves what needs to be re-examined in our corporate and private worship. What trends or liturgies (and we all have them) need to be let go, emptied so that Jesus can fill them with Himself and therefore be clearly and unmistakably seen? Maybe, just maybe, it's time to say confidently and honestly, "The old is gone; the new has come!"

- What aspects of your personal and corporate worship life could be re-examined and replaced with something fresh?
- What aspects seem full of life?

Notes...

10
Solid Foundations for Worship Leadership

❦ 1 Kings 3:4–9 ❧

*"You have continued this great kindness to him and
have given him a son to sit on his throne this very day."*
(1 Kings 3:6b)

King Solomon had a lot going for him, to say the least. We all know about his incredible wealth and his extraordinary wisdom. Unfortunately, we also know about his later years and how he got derailed and off track. But today's scripture passage demonstrates that, early on, Solomon seemed to know what it was that he didn't know. And more importantly, he knew where to go for help and answers. We can learn a lot by taking our cues from him, especially if we're in a leadership role in our worship ministry.

1. *A grateful heart* (verse 6) – It's easy to get caught up in the logistics and technicalities of worship leadership, focusing on what's wrong or what's missing or what's frustrating. Rather, try focusing on the incredible privilege we have in leading God's people in an encounter with Him. Be thankful for all those who give their time, energy, and resources to make this happen.

2. *A humble spirit* (verse 7) – Too many times we've seen leaders who've developed the mindset that it's all about them. None of us have gotten to where we are by ourselves. We're all the product of teachers, mentors, and those whose godly example has shaped us and helped us formulate our perspectives. We may have been given a platform, but we should never seek the spotlight.

3. *A servant attitude* (verses 8 & 9) – Let's face it: servant leadership is a rarity. Always has been, probably always will be. But Jesus provides us with a beautiful example of what a servant leader looks like. After all, everyone wants to feel needed, appreciated, and sometimes, just noticed.

Leadership is a privilege and a holy calling. Servanthood is the beautiful garment that marks a true leader.

Father, give us, like Solomon, discerning hearts, godly wisdom, and
servant attitudes. We are thankful for those whose example has
brought us to where we are today. Amen

- In what ways is servanthood a noticeable feature of your leadership style?
- In what ways can those features be enhanced?

Notes...

11
Inhabited or Inhibited?

❖ Mark 14:1–9 ❖

*"I tell you the truth, wherever the gospel is preached throughout
the world, what she has done will also be told, in memory of her."*
(Mark 14:9)

Mark 14 offers an interesting account that has altered my view of worship for several years now. You'll recall that Jesus was eating a meal with some friends when an unnamed woman (John's account identifies her as Mary) entered, broke open a container of expensive perfume, and then anointed Jesus with it. Monetarily, it was worth a year's wages! Imagine for a moment your annual income gone in about 20 seconds. Some who were standing by criticized her for "wasting" what could have been sold with the proceeds going to help the poor.

Today's key verse gives us Jesus' response. He said, in effect, "Leave her alone! She's done the proper thing, and her act of devotion will be remembered forever." And here we are in the twenty-first century talking about her. From this story, three principles come to mind that have shaped my own thoughts and planning of corporate worship:

- *Worship is expensive.* – This woman offered what the Bible says was worth a year's wages. We need to acknowledge that for us, too, worship will be costly. It costs time, energy, preparation, effort, and emotion. Yes, it's expensive—and worth it.

- *Worship is expressive.* – This dear woman could have waited until after the meal when everyone was gone and cornered Jesus alone to display her devotion. Instead, she acted without regard to others' reaction or judgment. We, too, need to worship freely, not according to public opinion or popular mandates, but according to His excellent greatness.

- *Worship is exalting.* – Exalting Jesus, that is. We're in danger these days of worshiping a style or a format, or even worship itself. Our goal is not to spotlight our specialness, but to lift up the Lamb.

Psalm 22 reminds us that God inhabits the praises of His people. If we do our part, I feel certain He'll do His. So, here's a good question: Is your worship *inhabited* or *inhibited?*

> *Dear Father, like this dear woman in scripture, we long to*
> *honor and adore You uninhibited. Give us a clear vision of*
> *Yourself so that we may honor You with all that we are. Amen*

- How much is your worship affected by popular opinion?
- To what extent are you willing to respond to God without fear of others' opinion?

Notes...

12
This Far

**Then King David went in and sat before the Lord, and he said:
"Who am I, O Sovereign Lord, and what is my family, that
you have brought me this far?"**
(2 Samuel 7:18)

Over and over, God's Word calls us to remember, to recall His mighty acts on our behalf. The ancient Israelites often set up stone altars to commemorate God's faithfulness to them. The prophet Samuel did this and even called it *Ebenezer*, saying, "This far has the Lord helped us" (1 Samuel 7:12).

In today's scripture reading, it's clear to see that David's response to God demonstrates the descriptions of him found in 1 Samuel 13:14 ("The Lord has sought out a man after his own heart") and in Psalm 17:8–9 (where his prayer was "Keep me as the apple of your eye; hide me in the shadow of your wings from the wicked who assail me, from my mortal enemies who surround me").

It's good to remember the "this fars" that God has brought us to. You see, His covenant always rests on *His* faithfulness, not ours. A realization of how far we've come results in intimacy, humility, regard for God's sovereignty, delight, and acknowledgment. Maybe that's what the apostle Paul was thinking when he wrote:

Oh, the depth of the riches of the wisdom and knowledge of God! How unsearchable his judgments, and his paths beyond tracing out! "Who has known the mind of the Lord? Or who has been his counselor? Who has ever given to God, that God should repay him?" For from him and through him and to him are all things. To him be the glory forever! (Romans 11:33–36)

Are you needing hope for tomorrow right now? Some reason to have faith for a bright future? Some assurance that God is still in control?

Sit back. Remember "This far."

*Oh, God, You are Sovereign over my yesterdays and Lord over
my tomorrows. "This far" You have led me and I trust You
for the path ahead. Amen*

- Have you taken time lately to just remember?
- What event can you recall that reminds you that God has helped you "this far"?
- How can your worship reflect this?

Notes...

13
An Attractive New Song

❖ Psalm 33:1–5 ❖

***Sing joyfully to the LORD, you righteous; it is fitting
for the upright to praise him.***
(Psalm 33:1)

Here's a truth you can count on: the worship of God by a group of believers who are sold out in their devotion to Him is one of the strongest forms of evangelism we have. Seekers who enter our churches are, by definition, *seeking something* they don't have. When they witness honest and whole-hearted responses to God, then the door is invitingly open for them to look into just what it is that this group has that they don't.

Today's key verse not only alludes to this truth, it affirms it: "it is fitting for the upright to praise him." I love the way the New American Standard Bible words this: "Sing for joy in the LORD, O you righteous ones; Praise is becoming to the upright." The Hebrew word rendered as "becoming" here is *na'veh*, meaning beautiful or seemly. (See also Psalm 147:1.) In other words, praise looks good on you! You're beautiful when you're praising God. And if you've ever stood before a gathering of honest worshipers, then you know this to be true.

Scripture includes so many references to "a new song" that it's impossible to ignore. Throughout history, when God's hand has moved on behalf of His people, the result has been a new song. You'll see this reality in Psalm 96:1–3, Psalm 144:9–14, Psalm 149:1–5, Isaiah 42:10–13, and ultimately in Revelation 5:6–9. A new song unleashes some significant truth, and it's always attractive!

Has God moved unmistakably in your life? Your response to Him will be noticed by those who are seeking an encounter with Him. So, sing your new song to Him with joy and with abandon.

And in case you didn't know it, you'll be looking pretty good when you do that!

*Father, You have moved so wonderfully, so powerfully, so
unmistakably in my life that I can't help but respond to You
in song. May my new song of praise to You bring You joy. Amen*

30

- How can worship be more attractive in your particular circumstance?
- What new song can you sing in response to what God has done?

14
More about that New Song

✦ Psalm 40:1–3 ✦

He put a new song in my mouth, a hymn of praise to our God.
Many will see and fear and put their trust in the Lord.
(Psalm 40:3)

Of all the things we can discern from reading about the experiences of King David, we can be certain of this: his life ran the gamut of emotions—from the highest praise to the deepest depression, it's all there. So too do his responses in these situations. Psalm 40 is a perfect example.

And who can't relate to this? Who hasn't felt like they're in a pit and that waiting on God is going to take a lifetime? But here's the key: how we respond to our pit is the hinge for other people's experience in worshiping God. David's story is certainly evidence of this.

As we know, throughout history, those who have experienced a mighty work of God in their lives have often responded with a "new song." And as we also know, that new song is an attractive way to draw others to Him. David, after being rescued from the pit and placed firmly on a rock to stand, says, "He put a new song in my mouth, a hymn of praise to our God."

It's interesting to note that the next line doesn't say, "Many will see and hear and put their trust in the Lord." It says, "Many will see and *fear* and put their trust in the Lord." The word for "fear" is *yare'*, and it can mean "to dread or to be afraid." But more importantly, it can also signify "to revere or to hold in reverence." It's very closely related to the word *yir'ah* in Proverbs 1:7, where we read "The fear of the Lord is the beginning of knowledge."

Your story can be a word of encouragement to those around you, and to those who are desperately seeking answers and frantically searching for the truth. So, tell it. Sing it.

Your new song has never sounded so beautiful.

Father, because You have rescued me, because You have
set my feet on a firm place to stand, I will sing to You my new song.
May it draw others into deep and reverent worship. Amen

- Does worship in your church inspire awestruck reverence of God?
- How can your story inspire others?

Notes...

15
Ministering To God

*At that time the Lord set apart the tribe of Levi to
carry the ark of the covenant of the Lord, to stand
before the Lord to minister and to pronounce blessings
in his name, as they still do today.*
(Deuteronomy 10:8)

Of all the duties and responsibilities given to the priests of Old Testament Israel (and there were a lot of them!), there seems to be one of primary importance: *ministering to God*. They were, of course, the official worship leaders, and they ministered to others, to be sure. But, as you can see reflected in 1 Chronicles 15:2 and 2 Chronicles 29:5 and 29:11, their very first priority was ministering to God.

This was the highest calling in the life of a priest. So, what does that look like for us? I like what Ephesians 5:10 endorses: "Find out what pleases the Lord"…then do it! That's a lifestyle guideline, of course, but it also applies to the way we approach and lead worship.

On a practical level, the act of ministering to God can take its direction from what Paul wrote in Ephesians 1:16–19:

I have not stopped giving thanks for you, remembering you in my prayers. I keep asking that the God of our Lord Jesus Christ, the glorious Father, may give you the Spirit of wisdom and revelation, so that you may know him better. I pray also that the eyes of your heart may be enlightened in order that you may know the hope to which he has called you, the riches of his glorious inheritance in the saints, and his incomparably great power for us who believe.

Where does that leave us? Here are a couple of principles we can glean from this: (1) God longs for us to come to Him because of what He can give us; (2) we're not saved for service; we're saved for a relationship; (3) don't substitute service, worship planning, or any other ministry tasks for the pursuit of God; and (4) don't make it your goal to learn more about God so much as you strive to know God. And remember, the

34

next time you're tempted to say, "This just doesn't minister to me; it doesn't meet my needs," it's not your needs we're talking about here.

Father, open our eyes to see You as we should. Open our ears to hear You. Open our hearts to receive You. Amen

- Does your service for God ever interfere with your relationship to God?
- How can you change that?

Notes...

16
Modern Day Priests

*But you are a chosen people, a royal priesthood, a holy
nation, a people belonging to God, that you may declare
the praises of him who called you out of darkness into his
wonderful light.*
(1 Peter 2:9)

Lots of us would say that we firmly believe in The Priesthood of All Believers, but what about The Priesthood of All Worship Team Members? Old Testament priests, as you'll remember, had lots of power, lots of authority, and lots of responsibility. And one of their primary responsibilities (after ministering to God) was leading the people in worship. Sometimes they spoke to the people on behalf of God, and sometimes they spoke to God on behalf of the people. They approached Him for their own needs, and they interceded for the sake of others. They declared "the praises of him who had called [them] out of darkness into his wonderful light." And, foreshadowing the affirmation of Isaiah 43:21, they did exactly what they were created to do.

Sounds a lot like our worship teams today, doesn't it?

It's true. As worship leaders, and "modern day priests" (according to Peter), we speak to the people on behalf of God, and we speak to God on behalf of the people. We intercede for each other, and we declare the praises of Him who created us and called us.

But just like our predecessors, our very first responsibility is ministering to God.

*Lord, we praise You for calling us into Your wonderful light. May the
words of our mouths and the meditations of our hearts bless You
and bring You joy. Amen*

- In what ways does your worship team speak to God on behalf of your congregation?
- In what ways do you speak to your people on behalf of God?
- Do the members of your worship team consider themselves to be "modern day priests"?

Notes...

17
Our Reward for Ministering to God

From now on all generations will call me blessed, for the
Mighty One has done great things for me—holy is his name.
(Luke 1:48b–49)

I first began seriously thinking about our first priority as worship leaders because I was concerned. I was concerned about our personal preferences and about popular opinion and about worship services that have become divisive because they've become identified by style. I was concerned that our "order of worship" might have become a "worship of order." And frankly, I was concerned about our concern over what *others* think of us, over what *we* think of us, and over what *God* thinks of us. Because (stay with me here) all these concerns indicate, deep down, what we think about God. To paraphrase A.W. Tozer, *what we think about God is the most important thought we have.*

If you read today's scripture passage (and I hope you did!), you saw Mary's response to the angel's announcement that she'd be the mother of the Messiah. She stated, "from now on all generations will call me blessed." That's from the root word *makarios*, meaning "supremely esteemed, of good fortune, happy." It's interesting, isn't it, that the high and mighty rarely seek God's help, so most of His work is done through those of less reputation. Mary's song of praise here, The Magnificat, is a good reminder that we, too, can praise *before* the promise is fulfilled.

And do you remember Anna, in Luke 2:36–38, who prayed daily in the temple and was rewarded with the privilege of beholding the Messiah? Anna paid attention, ministered to and listened to God, and reminds us that none of us should walk where we haven't prayed. And those Levites in Deuteronomy 10:9 and 18:2? Their reward, their inheritance, wasn't a plot of real estate like all the other tribes of Israel.

Their reward, their inheritance, was God Himself.

Lord, as we minister to You, and as we minister to Your people,
remind us that You are our very great reward. Keep us mindful
of our very first priority. Amen

- In what ways, or in what situations, can you praise God before the promise is fulfilled?
- What's stopping you from doing that?

Notes…

18
What God Expects

❁ Psalm 150 ❁

Praise Him for His mighty deeds;
Praise Him according to His excellent greatness.
(Psalm 150:2 NASB)

I've got friends who ask for advice, but what they really want is affirmation. They ask for guidance, but they're really looking for confirmation. You may have friends like this, too. They say things like, "I see what you're saying, but don't you think ..." or "Oh, I understand, but I was thinking ...." It gets a little tiring, doesn't it?

God doesn't operate like this, and He doesn't look for us to respond like this. Did you know He has certain expectations when it comes to the way we worship Him? For instance, Jesus said that the Father is looking for *worshipers* (you and me) who will worship Him in spirit and in truth (see John 4). He's not looking for a program, a style, a particular architecture, flamboyant personalities, or even the newest song. He's looking for *us*, and His expectation is that we'll worship Him with a clean, pure, and open attitude in a manner that's consistent with and based on His word, the truth that scripture affords.

And He expects us to worship Him "according to His excellent greatness." Not according to personal preference or popular opinion. *According to* who He is and all He's done. When we see "according to" in scripture, it usually indicates "out of," "in relation to," "because of," or "in proportion to." It has nothing to do with what *I* was thinking or what *you* were thinking.

It has everything to do with who *He* is and what *He's* done.

Sovereign God, Your greatness is beyond our understanding and
greater than our comprehension. We will worship You according
to all You are and all You've done. Amen

- Do you think there's any limit to God's excellent greatness?
- Personally, how can you praise Him according to, or in relation to, His excellent greatness?

Notes…

19
Your Everythingness

*Hear, O Israel: The L*ORD *our God, the L*ORD *is one.*
*Love the L*ORD *your God with all your heart and with*
all your soul and with all your strength.
(Deuteronomy 6:4–5)

Jesus, being the good Rabbi and observant Jew that He was, knew exactly where to turn when He was asked what was the greatest commandment of them all. You can see for yourself His answer in Mark 12:29–30. His reply was based on Deuteronomy 6:4–5, the ultimate motivation for worship, the battle cry of Israel.

This passage would have been familiar to both the questioners of Jesus and those who happened to be standing close by. It was referred to as the *Shema,* since that was the first word in the passage (translated "Hear"), meaning to listen in the sense of obeying. This was and is the central tenet of monotheism. As usual, Jesus expanded the meaning to something beyond a statement of faith. He turned it into a call to worship.

It's helpful to know that the Greek word that Jesus used in the Mark 12 passage, translated as "strength," is *iskoos* or *ischus.* We don't really have an exact parallel English word for it, but if we did, it would be something like "everythingness." What Jesus was saying is that our worship of God is to be much more than just mental ascent, more than simply proclaiming a set of beliefs, more than being satisfied that we've aligned ourselves with theological orthodoxy. These are important things and vital to us if we're going to worship "in spirit and in truth." But here Jesus is calling for even more. For *all,* actually.

Jesus' words demand a response—a response to God for all He is and for all He's done. It's a response of everything that's in us. After all, that's what worship is: a response. We didn't make it up, and we can't really initiate it. We can only respond.

And there are plenty of reasons to do that.

Father, today we offer You all we are and all we have because
of all You are and all You've done. You are our God and we
are Your people. Amen

- How does holding to a set of beliefs differ from responding whole-heartedly to God?
- How is each (believing and responding) vital?

Notes...

20
A Little Perspective, Please

⚘ Ezra 3:8–13 ⚘

No one could distinguish the sound of the shouts of joy from
the sound of weeping, because the people made so much noise.
And the sound was heard far away.
(Ezra 3:13)

I have to credit my pastor, Dr. Dan Burnett, with the idea for this devotional. If you're like me, you're grateful for a pastor who consistently brings a word from God's truth in a practical, applicable way. But first, a little backstory concerning today's scripture passage.

Ezra and his fellow captives have been granted permission to return from their Persian exile, in order to rebuild the temple in Jerusalem. Assignments have been made, and the construction workers have busily begun their tasks. Once the foundation has been laid, excitement builds to the point where a worship celebration breaks out. An orchestra accompanies shouts and songs of praise, and everyone is ecstatic!

Well…almost everyone.

You see, some of those who had returned also remembered the former glory of the former temple. They were well along in years and had witnessed the horror of their beloved house of worship being destroyed. Others, younger and probably born while Israel was in exile, were simply thrilled at the prospect of creating something to honor their God. To them, this "rebuilding" was a first-time experience.

"This is fantastic!" cried the younger ones.

"It's just not the same," lamented the older ones.

It was history versus modern ideas. It was tradition versus new paradigms. It was the generation of experience versus the generation of possibilities. It was a little (or maybe a lot) like hymnals versus projected lyrics, pipe organs versus electric guitars, or traditional hymns with their deep theology versus modern worship songs with their fresh expression.

Listen, both views are valid and both views are needed. It's a matter of perspective, and when tradition melds with possibility, the results can be fathomless.

Lord, Your greatness is beyond our stylistic preferences and any of
our traditions. Give us the grace to accept each other as we seek
to honor you in unity. Amen

- In what ways can tradition and newer expressions clash?
- In what ways can they meld?

Notes...

21
Preventive Medicine

***In his distress he sought the favor of the L*ORD *his God
and humbled himself greatly before the God of his fathers.***
(2 Chronicles 33:12)

It lies at the root of many of our disagreements. It's the origin of many a person's downfall. It's the genesis of the destruction of too many lives to number. Sometimes, it's diagnosed as ambition. On other occasions, it cloaks itself as self-assertion. Then there are instances where it's labeled as a strong work ethic. But all of these are lies.

It's pride, and God's Word condemns it. God's Word also warns against it.

When pride comes, then comes disgrace, but with humility comes wisdom.
(Proverbs 11:2)
Pride goes before destruction, a haughty spirit before a fall.
(Proverbs 16:18)
A man's pride brings him low, but a man of lowly spirit gains honor.
(Proverbs 29:23)
...those who walk in pride he is able to humble.
(Daniel 4:37)

It's a subtle and seductive thing, and those who have any sort of public, up-front image are prone to feel it tugging at the ego. Someone hints to us that we're the next greatest thing and suddenly, in our minds, we are, in fact, the next greatest thing. The sad fact is that musicians in the Church are especially vulnerable to this. Music, by its very nature, is "performance" oriented, and performance often leads to comparison or to competition. Then what was once an honorable offering of worship to God becomes infected with the overwhelming desire to be noticed.

Now, ambition, self-assertion, and a strong work ethic aren't necessarily bad things. In fact, scripture also warns against laziness and idleness. These become infections, though, when they mask the desire for attention, the craving for respect, or the insatiable hunger to be the object of envy. And infections lead to diseases. A little preventive medicine would be a good thing.

46

- What steps can you take to be sure that pride has no place in your ministry and in your personal life?
- What's the difference between self-respect and pride?

Notes...

22
What If

❧ Psalm 100 ❧

Enter his gates with thanksgiving and his courts with praise;
give thanks to him and praise his name.
(Psalm 100:4)

What if, just for this Sunday, when we entered our place of worship, we didn't sing to try to impress anyone (or we didn't refrain from singing because we felt intimidated), but instead we offered up a shout of joy to the Lord?

What if, instead of grumbling or complaining about parking, technical issues, lack of attendance, or any number of physical distractions that could derail us, we truly worshiped the Lord with gladness?

What if, in place of a litany of our current, past, or presumed future woes, trials, and tribulations, we came before God not with a lament, but with joyful songs?

And what if, just for this Sunday, we replaced our illusory sense of self-sufficiency, our exaggerated sense of accomplishment, and our self-deceiving sense of importance, and we came to realize that the Lord, *He* is God, not us. We're His creation, His people, His sheep.

Then, what if we determined that we'd abandon all efforts at comparison, we'd give up dwelling on what we don't have, and we'd enter His gates with thanksgiving…for all He is and for all He's done? What if our thankfulness then turned to spontaneous praise?

Just for this Sunday, what if we intentionally made no comment about or reference to the results of the previous day's sporting events, and we engaged in no discussions as to what the rest of this day holds, but we gave thanks for this very moment, and we blessed His name?

What if we spent the entire day resting in the goodness of the Lord, kicking back in the assurance that His love is not just for today, but for eternity?

And what if we could impart this assurance to someone of a younger generation who needs to see and hear how faith in God is lived out, how the righteous have never been forsaken?

Just for this Sunday…what if?

Father God, today we choose to focus on Your goodness, Your love, Your faithfulness. Today we choose to focus on You, and we bless Your name. Amen

- Seriously, how would worship in your church be different if these suggestions were taken to heart?
- How would you be changed?

Notes...

23
Someone's Always Listening

About midnight Paul and Silas were praying and singing hymns to
God, and the other prisoners were listening to them.
(Acts 16:25)

Picture it with me for a moment: Paul and Silas are ministering in Philippi, witnessing a number of conversions as the result of their preaching. The owners of a demon-possessed, fortune-telling girl become distressed when Paul casts the demon from her. You see, suddenly these slave owners realize their source of income is slipping away. All this leads quickly to an arrest, and Paul and Silas are beaten, shackled, and thrown into prison.

About midnight, still in prison and still in chains, still under arrest for preaching the gospel, Paul and Silas begin, of all things, singing! Can you imagine? Hymns of praise right in the middle of deep despair! A worship service despite their cruel and unfair treatment! Singing jailbirds accompanied by clinking chains and the pain of a flogging!

There's a short line in verse 25 of today's reading that's often overlooked: "the other prisoners were listening to them." Just like that, Paul and Silas turn an invitation for pity into an opportunity for testimony. And someone was listening. Someone's always listening.

So, how would you respond if you were the subject of this story? How do you, in fact, respond when crisis occurs?

- When you're unfairly criticized?
- When your company downsizes and you're part of the cut?
- When your work goes unrecognized and unappreciated?
- When that relationship is broken?
- When the diagnosis is terminal?

Our worship in these life-shattering moments reveals a lot about where our faith is deposited, and in Whom our trust is invested.

And believe me, someone's always listening.

- Have you ever been given the chance to turn an invitation for pity into an opportunity for testimony?
- What can you do to prepare for such a situation?

Notes...

24
Landmarks...Don't Miss Them

✤ 1 Corinthians 15:1–8 ✤

For what I received I passed on to you as of first importance:
that Christ died for our sins according to the Scriptures, that he was buried,
that he was raised on the third day according to the Scriptures.
(1 Corinthians 15:3–4)

If you're involved in the music and worship ministry of your church, then you know all too well that things don't just happen. They take planning, preparation, and rehearsal. If it's November, then you're up to your eyeballs in Christmas preparations, but you're also thinking about Easter. If it's March, then Easter plans are well underway, but you're also considering what the summer months might look like.

And so it goes, season by season, year after year.

We Christians are a commemorating and celebrating bunch. Every time we gather for worship, we recall the mighty act of redemption on our behalf, and we joyfully respond in praise and thanksgiving. That's what we do best and, really, it's what we should do most. That's putting first things first. And since we've mentioned seasons, let's talk about Easter for a moment.

Look again at today's key verse taken from Paul's epic writing in 1 Corinthians 15. That's it! That's the gospel—the death, burial, and resurrection of Jesus. And at Easter, we have an especially opportune time to share this gospel with our world. But it takes preparation, both personally and among those with whom we serve. The road to Easter's triumph is full of significant landmarks along the way. Be sure you don't miss them:

Watch for the joyful exuberance of Palm Sunday.
Look for the tender, compassionate encounters of Jesus' final week.
Search for the significance of the Last Supper.
Hear the garden pleadings of our Savior's agonized prayer.
Relive the humiliation, torture, and death of the Messiah.
Feel again the despair of a world gone dark, the Light of the World extinguished.

Then, just maybe, by God's grace, we'll be ready for Easter Sunday.

*Oh Jesus, we anticipate the joy and celebration that Easter Sunday brings.
But this year, give us the grace to see and to hear and to feel what You
endured for us. Amen*

- What significant landmarks for worship do you see in this current season?
- How are you preparing?

Notes...

25
The Posture of Worship

***Shout with joy to God, all the earth! Sing the glory
of his name; make his praise glorious!***
(Psalm 66:1–2)

Worship is such a physical activity…or at least it should be! Just consider Psalm 66, for example, and all its assertions concerning bodily gestures. We're encouraged to shout, to sing, to speak, and to bow. The Bible never prompts us to worship in a passive, observant way. No, if its commands were followed fully, we'd probably wind up exhausted. But then, we *are* worshiping the King of Creation and the Lord of the Universe.

You have to wonder, though, if we're missing something; if we're a little too familiar with the words we read; if we haven't, through repetition, watered down the text just a bit.

Today's scripture passage is a prime example of this. The word we read, "shout" or "shout joyfully," comes from the Hebrew word *ruwa*, and it means (get this!) "to split the ears with sound" or "to sound aloud an alarm." We're not talking about a feeble, half-voiced utterance here. We're talking about (I'll say it again) *splitting the ears with sound*. And it doesn't seem to be a suggestion. It appears to be a command.

Or consider the little word "say" in verse 3 of Psalm 66. That's *amar*, and it signifies "an indisputable declaration, a determined proclamation or report." After all, we're addressing royalty, you know.

All this is echoed in Psalm 47:

*Clap your hands, all you nations; shout to God with cries of joy…
Sing praises to God, sing praises; sing praises to our King, sing praises.*

For now, one more word on gestures. Psalm 95:6 implores us, "Come, let us bow down in worship, let us kneel before the LORD our Maker." The Hebrew words for "bow down" and "kneel" both imply "bending the knee in blessing; to lie face down; to prostrate oneself."

Maybe it's time that our ushers began handing out Sunday bulletins and yoga mats! Ultimately, though, it's not our physical posture that counts. It's the posture of our heart.

54

- How physical is your worship?
- Why?

Notes...

26
Jehoshaphat's Strategy

♦ 2 Chronicles 20:15–21 ♦

After consulting the people, Jehoshaphat appointed men to sing to the Lord and to praise him for the splendor of his holiness as they went out at the head of the army, saying: "Give thanks to the Lord, for his love endures forever."
(2 Chronicles 20:21)

You remember the story, don't you? Jehoshaphat, king of Judah, has just been informed that he and his kingdom are being surrounded by not one, not two, but three aggressive armies. On the surface, things look grim (as in annihilation is certain). When he hears this, he employs a unique strategy that is not at all expected.

First, he prays. We'll talk more about this in the next reading, but for now let's take notice that this was Jehoshaphat's first course of action. It wasn't a last resort of "All we can do now is pray." Seeking God was primary in his strategic arsenal.

Second, he gathers the people of Judah together for, of all things, more prayer along with fasting. He doesn't gather the Joint Chiefs of Staff, or the brightest military strategists of the day, but instead he implores the commoners, folks a lot like you and me, to seek the face of God.

Then, Jahaziel, one of the Levites, speaks up with a prophetic word of encouragement, and he tells Jehoshaphat not to be afraid or discouraged because the battle is not his, but God's (see verse 15 of today's reading). He should go face the enemy, and God will be with him (verse 17). We're not always going to understand everything we face, you know. Our job is to accept these things, stand firm, and watch God work (see Exodus 14:14 and Deuteronomy 20:4).

Finally, as Jehoshaphat sends out his army for battle, he does the craziest thing—he places the choir at the head of his advancing troops! (Actually, this may say more about what he thought of the choir, but that's a discussion for later.) At any rate, the choir leads the army out, singing as they go: "Give thanks to the Lord, for his love endures forever."

I see the unity and power of a choir here, as they remind the army of just where their ultimate allegiance is. And I see opportunity for service for those who are skilled, gifted, and passionate about the musical arts. And that's true for us today, isn't it? There's an unmistakable power when singers come together in unity. And there's a distinct reason Jehoshaphat placed his choir where he did, and we'll talk more about that next time.

Lord God, Your love endures forever. We thank and praise You
for Your power in our lives. Amen

- Do you see the potential for power and unity in a choir in worship?
- How would you describe that?

Notes...

27
Jehoshaphat's Victory

❖ 2 Chronicles 20:5–7, 20:12, 20:22–23 ❖

"We do not know what to do, but our eyes are upon you."
(2 Chronicles 20:12c)

If you read all of today's suggested scripture verses (and I hope you will!), you'll see again King Jehoshaphat's reliance on prayer as a prime military strategy. You'll see, too, that the result of prayer and praise, used in strategic fashion, was a stunning victory for Jehoshaphat. Actually, it was God's victory because, as you'll recall from the previous reading, we're not called to understand, but to accept, to stand firm, and to watch God work.

Want a spiritual principle for this? Here it is: *Praise goes before the battle.* And that's especially true where spiritual warfare is concerned. After all, we're not battling flesh and blood most of the time. We're fighting rulers, authorities, powers, and spiritual forces in the heavenly realms (see Ephesians 6:10–12).

We can praise God because we have assurance. We have assurance because of our history with Him. 2 Chronicles 20 is a good reminder of this. Look again at Jehoshaphat's prayer.

Verse 6: "O Lord, God of our fathers, *are you not* the God who is in heaven?" That's trust in God for our present need.

Verse 7: "O our God, *did you not* drive out the inhabitants of this land…" That's trust in God because of our past need.

Verse 12: "O our God, *will you not* judge them?" That's trust in God for our future need.

It's just as true for you today, my friend. Whatever you're facing, praise goes before the battle.

O God, You are our strength and our song,
the same yesterday, today, and tomorrow. Amen

58

- What are you facing today that needs to be addressed first of all with praise?
- How could your church adopt this sort of spiritual strategy?

28
Godly Interruptions

❖ Luke 7:11–17 ❖

*Then he went up and touched the coffin, and those carrying it
stood still. He said, "Young man, I say to you, get up!"*
(Luke 7:14)

I know, I know. You're as busy as you can possibly be today, and tomorrow looks even busier. The last thing in the world you need is an interruption to derail you from your agenda.

I've lived there. Some days, I feel like I'm still living there. But lately, I've been praying about how to embrace the interruptions. And sure enough, God seems to delight in answering that prayer…with interruptions. But here's one thing that I've learned: the interruption can be where God does some of His most spectacular work.

If you haven't already, familiarize yourself again with the story in Luke 7:11–17. Jesus is having what appears to be a fairly busy day. He's surrounded by His disciples and a large crowd. By all appearances, He's on His way to minister in a town called Nain.

Then, the interruption occurs. He's met by a funeral procession at the town gate. The dead person being carried out is the only son of a widow. We don't know his age precisely, but Jesus eventually calls him, "young man." Could it have been a child?

"When the Lord saw [the mother], his heart went out to her…" (verse 13). The Greek word employed here by Luke is *splagchnizomai*, meaning "to feel deeply, to yearn, to have compassion and pity." It's as if Jesus was thinking, "This isn't the way it's supposed to be." Then, He does an astounding thing. He walks up, touches the coffin, commands the young man to rise, and a resurrection occurs! Now understand this: no self-respecting Jew would ever—I mean *ever*—touch a coffin that contains a dead person. To do so would be total defilement. Yet, that's what Jesus does; He touches (*haptomai*: to connect or bind, to apply oneself to) and new life occurs.

Look, I know you're busy. And much of that busyness probably centers on the work of your church. But can I challenge you to embrace today's interruptions? To "apply yourself" to some person or some situation?

Who knows, new life just might occur.

- What interruptions have you faced recently?
- Are you prepared to embrace today's interruptions?

Notes...

29
It's Just a Name

✦ Romans 16:1–16 ✦

Greet Rufus, chosen in the Lord, and his mother,
who has been a mother to me, too.
(Romans 16:13)

OK, let's just admit it. Isn't this about the dullest passage of scripture you've read in a while? It's just a list of names—and difficult-to-pronounce names at that! Andronicus, Asyncritus, Stachys, Philologus—what were their mothers thinking?

Except that these names represent people. Real people. People who had helped Paul and made a significant impact on his life.

> Priscilla and Aquila—they risked their lives for him.
> Andronicus and Junias—they were in prison with him.
> Urbanus—he was a fellow worker in Christ.
> Apelles—he was tested and approved in Christ.
> Tryphena and Tryphosa—they were hard workers in the Lord.

The list goes on, including "Rufus, chosen in the Lord, and his mother, who [had] been a mother to [Paul], too."

You have a list like this, too. You may not have written it down, but I'm guessing you could if you tried. Your list, like mine, would include those who helped start you on your journey of faith, those who encouraged you as you entered your place of service, and those who supported you spiritually, emotionally, or financially. Your list might also include those who stood by you in tough times due to outside causes or even your own foolish choices. Maybe they didn't risk their life for you, but they risked their reputation.

Can you see them? Can you see your list of names? Those names represent important people in your life, and I'm wondering if you've thanked them lately.

Lord Jesus, how grateful we are for the people who have invested
greatly in our lives. May we be just as supportive to others who
may need us. Amen

- Who would be on your list of significant people who have helped you along your journey of faith?
- When was the last time you thanked them?

Notes…

30
Marks of a Good Leader

And the Lord told him: "Listen to all that the people are saying to you;
it is not you they have rejected, but they have rejected me as their king.
(1 Samuel 8:7)

Samuel had a tough job. As prophet to and judge over Israel, he imparted the words of God to a sometimes stubborn and cantankerous people. But this was nothing new to him. You'll recall that he was called by God as he ministered before Him under Eli the priest. Soon enough Samuel was recognized as a powerful prophet and his words were revered.

Decades later, Israel wants a king rather than continuing to be led by prophets and judges as God had ordained. Apparently, all the other nations were ruled this way, and in their minds, that's the way it should be done in Israel, too. How dangerous it is to compare ourselves to others rather than to remain content in the calling God has placed on our lives.

The rest of the saga is well known, and you can refresh your memory by reading 1 Samuel 10:9–19. Saul is anointed as king, though clearly it's a mistake and totally not what God had desired for His chosen people. Through it all, Samuel demonstrated some unique marks of a good leader, and I think these characteristics provide some good principles for us today.

- Samuel was secure in his calling. He fulfilled his obligations despite continued protest.
- He was willing to share authority. He appointed judges for the people, as indicated in the first verse of chapter 8.
- He was eager to help others develop their potential. He even took part in the coronation of Saul.
- Samuel was a truth speaker. Despite popular opinion, he was unremitting in proclaiming God's Word.
- He had a heart for God and for God's people. He only wanted the best for them… God's best.

We can learn a lot from Samuel. And we'd do well to remember that often when God doesn't give us what we want, it's because He knows what our desires would cost us.

O God, give us the spirit and the courage of Samuel. May Your truth be the truth we impart to those we lead. Amen

- How can Samuel's leadership style impact the way you lead and serve others?
- Have you ever faced challenges that caused you to question your calling?

Notes...

31
A Sacrifice of Praise

❧ Hebrews 13:11–16 ❧

Through Jesus, therefore, let us continually offer to God
a sacrifice of praise—the fruit of lips that confess his name.
(Hebrews 13:15)

The book of Hebrews talks a lot about covenants and sacrifices. It was, after all, written to a group of Jewish believers, and they would have been very familiar with both concepts. They would have been well aware that their covenants with God would require of them both allegiance and sacrifice.

And that's pretty much the point of this theologically rich and deeply significant portion of our Bible, only with a twist. What these readers' parents, grandparents, great-grandparents, and great-great-grandparents had observed and practiced for generations was, in fact, symbolic. All the ancient rituals of worship prescribed by the law, in actuality, pointed to Christ, the ultimate sacrifice and the mediator of the new covenant. Old Testament sacrifices were offered in the covenant name of Yahweh. Our sacrifices today, says the writer of Hebrews, are offered in the name of Jesus, the Messiah.

It's quite possible that some of those who read or heard this letter for the first time, and especially this portion of the letter, recalled the words of Psalm 107:22: "Let them sacrifice thank offerings and tell of [God's] works with songs of joy."

Or maybe they would have flashed back on Hosea 14:2: "Say to [God]: 'Forgive all our sins and receive us graciously, that we may offer the fruit of our lips.' "

A sacrifice requires something of us: our best. It demands to be thought out, not a remnant or a leftover, but the "first fruits." If praise is to be our sacrifice, then it's also to be a priority.

Lord, may our words of praise be a sacrificial offering to You. We
hold back nothing because You gave everything. Amen

- How much are you willing to sacrifice in order to make worship a priority?
- Are you willing to make this a daily discipline?

32
Stand in Awe of God

Much dreaming and many words are meaningless.
Therefore stand in awe of God.
(Ecclesiastes 5:7)

There's a real tension in worship, and it's never been felt more acutely than today. How do we balance intimacy *with* God with reverence *for* God? How can we speak and sing of Him as a Friend, when He's the Creator and sovereign King of the universe? When we reference His great love and mercy, do we also remind ourselves of His call to repentance and sacrifice in our lives?

Our worship of God is at its best when our understanding of God is at its fullest (not that any of us could ever fully fathom His essence. Besides, who wants a God we can totally grasp?). The more we know of Him—the more we *know Him*—the more appropriate our response in worship will be.

That's why what we speak and sing in worship is vital and worthy of close examination. You'll remember how Job was chastised for speaking things about God's character and activity when, as God reminded him, he really had no inkling of what he was talking about. If you're a worship leader, then you know what a formidable responsibility it is to put words in the mouths of your people. What they speak and sing will be with them for a long, long time, often even after other mental faculties are all but gone. *So, be careful what you say*, says Solomon, the writer of Ecclesiastes. *You speak for eternity.*

In the end, God is bigger than our descriptions. He's broader than our questions. And He's beyond our imaginations.

So, let your words be few.

Stand in awe of God.

O God, our understanding of you is so limited, yet You are limitless.
Nothing we could say would be adequate to describe all You are.
Receive, then, our silent praise. Amen

- How do you balance intimacy *with* God with reverence *for* God?
- How thoughtful are you concerning the words you use in worship?

Notes...

33
Make It Count

May the words of my mouth and the meditation of my heart
be pleasing in your sight, O Lord, my Rock and my Redeemer.
(Psalm 19:14)

Words and music both play an integral part in worship. Sometimes, they're employed separately. At other times, they're incorporated together as one entity. We call these songs, hymns, or anthems.

There's a reason why, for centuries, military units have included bands, or at least a fife and drum corps, among their ranks. And what is it about a school fight song (accompanied by cheerleaders, the pep squad, and a stadium full of fanatics) that pumps us up? Both of these stir up an allegiance and inspire a dedication without us even having to think about it.

No doubt, there's a power in the music we choose and in the songs we sing. Music can be one of the most potent tools we have for teaching truth and expressing faith. Think of it this way: just as an IV solution opens up our veins so that medicine can be pumped into us, music (and other art forms) opens up our heart so that a vital message can be easily absorbed. A saline solution with no medicine to follow leaves us vulnerable. A strong melody or infectious rhythm with no truth attached (or worse yet, a damaging message attached) can be detrimental to our spiritual health.

And what about the words we use in worship? I have a friend who says that the very first rule of public speaking is *have something to say*. That's advice worth taking to heart, but it's a concept that, I fear, we don't consider strongly enough. For instance, the opening words for worship have power—power to engage our congregation and focus attention on God. Likewise, they have the power to be disengaging when trivial or lacking focus.

If you're involved in worship leadership at all, this Sunday, how will you invite people to worship? Take Psalm 19 as your cue. Like many other Psalms, it gives us a vision of God we don't see every day. The point is this: before the day is done, our congregations will hear plenty of "Good to see ya!" and "How ya doin'?" We have one chance to set the tone and direct the focus of worship.

Let's make it count.

- Whatever your role in worship leadership, have you considered the impact of the words you use?
- How can you eliminate the trivial and elevate the sublime?

Notes…

34
Worship Demands a Response

❖ Isaiah 6:1–8 ❖

*Then I heard the voice of the L*ORD *saying, "Whom shall I send?
And who will go for us?" And I said, "Here am I. Send me!"*
(Isaiah 6:8)

The opening verses of Isaiah 6 are well known and have been the basis for countless sermons and songs that focus on worship, and rightly so! The vivid imagery portrayed here reminds us that worship is more than just what we know about God. It must embrace all that we don't know—His greatness, His vastness, His holiness.

Isaiah sees the LORD enthroned, exalted high with the train of His robe filling the temple. In ancient times, the length of the train of a king's robe often indicated the breadth of the king's empire, the depth of his authority, and the expanse of the kingdoms he had conquered. In this case, the train of God's robe filled the entire temple! And He's called "holy" (*qadosh*) not once, but three times, which in the Hebrew idiom denotes a superlative degree or totality. He is *Elohim Kedoshim* (Holy God), and holiness is the sum of all His attributes.

Isaiah's vision of and encounter with God leave him shaken; "ruined" or "undone" is how he described himself. He had seen the LORD Almighty, and deep humility was his only proper response to God as he now saw his sin in light of God's holiness. And that's not all. Isaiah's lips—his instrument of service—were touched by live coals taken from the altar. You may recall that burning coals of fire were taken by a priest into the Holy of Holies on the Day of Atonement as part of the sacrifice to atone for the sins of the people. Once the burning coals touched Isaiah's lips, it was declared that his sin had been atoned for and his guilt removed.

But he's not finished yet. In fact, he's commissioned. God speaks: "Whom shall I send? And who will go for us?" And Isaiah responds by accepting the call.

Worship doesn't end when the service is over. Worship isn't concluded when we walk out the doors. If we leave unchanged, uninspired, unmotivated, we've missed a major point of the whole encounter.

Worship demands a response.

- Are you ever tempted to leave worship behind you as you exit the doors of your church?
- How can you carry that experience into your world?

Notes...

35
Pay Attention, Please

❖ Luke 24:13–32 ❖

They asked each other, "Were not our hearts burning within us
while he talked with us on the road and opened the Scriptures to us?"
(Luke 24:32)

God can, and does, work around our physical laws. He created it all; He can do with it as He pleases. And sometimes, He works through ordinary events with extraordinary timing to carry out His purposes. Those who lean toward self-sufficiency seem to rarely seek God's help. And so, many times, His work is fulfilled through those with less reputation and visibility—those you might least expect, but those who were paying attention.

The first two chapters of Luke's gospel are an amazing study in those who were listening and expecting. Zechariah paid attention, worked through his doubting, and became the father of John the Baptist. His wife, Elizabeth, acknowledged God as the One who blessed her with great honor. Mary, the mother of our Lord, paid attention, received the message of the angel Gabriel, and birthed the Messiah. Simeon was paying attention when he sensed the presence of the Lord's Christ right beside him in the temple courts. Then there's Anna, the prophetess, who knew for certain who that Child was, and she spoke words of blessing over Him.

How often Jesus appears—walking right beside us, in our trials, even in our worship!—and we don't recognize Him. Why is that? Are we too self-centered? Too focused on our problems? Too concerned with technicalities and logistics? Disinterested? How foolish we are! The word translated as "explained" in today's passage actually means *to translate with excitement and authority*. How do you like that! I'm sensing that Jesus really does want to explain the things that puzzle us, that confuse us, that perplex us. We just have to listen. We have to pay attention.

It's easy for us in the twenty-first century to look back at these stories from scripture and marvel at how the people seemed to have missed it all. But after all this time, we really haven't changed much. In the middle of today's frantic pace, how often we totally miss God's activity in and around us because we just aren't paying attention. We wait for God to act as we think He should, and He moves in a way that seems to come out of the cosmic left field. Or worse, we feel like He hasn't acted at all. We get frustrated, confused, discouraged…angry.

And we miss it.

Speak, Lord, for Your people are listening. Amen

- Do you ever sense that God is trying to speak to you? How?
- Are you willing to quiet your spirit enough so that you can pay attention and hear Him?

Notes…

36
For His Glory, For His Pleasure

❖ Revelation 4:1–11 ❖

"Holy, holy, holy is the Lord God Almighty,
who was, and is, and is to come."
(Revelation 4:8b)

Most of us sing, or have sung in some form for most of our lives, the phrase "Praise Him above, ye heavenly host" from the Doxology. What a poignant reminder that when we gather for corporate worship, we don't do it alone and we don't really initiate anything. What we do is "plug in" to what scripture says is an ongoing, never-ending, everlasting worship experience at the throne of the Lamb. I guess, in a way, that we're rehearsing now on earth what we'll be doing throughout eternity. I guess, too, that we'd better start really loving those around us—we're going to spend a long, long time with them!

In chapter 4 of the book of Revelation, "the throne" is central because nothing can be understood apart from its relationship to Jesus, the Lamb, the One seated on it. The throne is, clearly, in heaven (verse 2); encircled by a rainbow, the symbol of God's faithfulness (verse 3); and a focal point of worship (verses 4, 6, and 10). From it come flashes of lightning, as well as peals of thunder, and before it, seven lamps are blazing, representing fullness, completion, or perfection (verse 5).

All this is reminiscent of chapter 6 of Isaiah's prophecy, especially with the eternal anthem that's recorded in today's key verse. We're reminded that in this instance "holy," repeated three times, represents God's totality, His completeness. God's holiness isn't merely another of His attributes (as though "merely" could describe any of His attributes!). Holiness is God's essence; it's what sets Him apart; it's what makes Him "other."

In heaven, as it should be on earth, God is worshiped for who He is (verse 8) and for what He's done (verse 11): "You are worthy, our Lord and God, to receive glory and honor and power, for you created all things, and by your will they were created and have their being." The King James Version renders the latter part of this verse as "and for thy pleasure they are and were created."

On a personal level, concerning our own lives, it's probably worth asking ourselves (and you can fill in the blank): "Does _________ bring God glory? Does _________ bring Him pleasure?"

Lord God Almighty, may our worship bring You glory and our
actions bring You pleasure. You alone are holy. Amen

- Does worship in your congregation honor God for who He is, as well as for what He's done?
- Does it bring Him glory? Does it bring Him pleasure?

Notes…

37
His Joy, Our Strength

❧ Nehemiah 8:1–12 ❧

*This day is sacred to our Lord. Do not grieve, for the
joy of the Lord is your strength.*
(Nehemiah 8:10b)

In case no one has told you, it's OK to celebrate. It's perfectly acceptable to be joyful. And despite what you may have been taught, Christians *can* have fun, and worship *can* be characterized by exuberance. Just ask Ezra or Nehemiah.

I hope you've read all of today's scripture reading because there are a few things that deserve some attention. From what we understand historically, this gathering would have involved everybody, women and children included. This was important, and this would have an impact on future generations, so everyone was there.

Ezra the priest read to them "the Law" (verse 2), which probably included the first five books of our Bible, but most certainly included the books of Exodus, Leviticus, and Deuteronomy. I know you're thinking it, so I'll go ahead and say it: Ezra laid down the law.

Please don't miss the phrase "from daybreak till noon" in verse 3. Ezra read the Word of God to the people from daybreak till noon. That's in the range of six hours, conservatively speaking. And since most of those in attendance would have had no access to the scrolls, if they could even read at all, they listened for about six hours. Then, they had a party. They had a party because they had heard, and now understood, the Law of God. They celebrated with joy since the joy of the Lord, as Nehemiah told them, was to be their strength.

We'd probably all consider ourselves and our congregations to be "people of the Word." Yet, it can be a little disheartening to discover how, in some cases, the reading of scripture is relegated to a minor, barely-there experience. When the Word of God is incorporated in significant, meaningful ways in our worship, there's power and there's joy. The joy of the Lord, our strength.

*O Lord, Your Word is precious to us, a lamp to our feet and a
light to our path. Forgive us when we've neglected Your Word,
and fill us with joy—Your joy, our strength. Amen*

- Does the reading of God's Word have a significant place in the worship life of your congregation?
- How big a role does it play in your private worship?

Notes…

38
Extravagance

※ Matthew 27:45–54 ※

At that moment the curtain of the temple was torn in two
from top to bottom. The earth shook and the rocks split.
(Matthew 27:51)

Some events call for extravagance. Take, for example, when Jesus was born. That scenario was preceded by at least three angelic visitations, and some humble, unassuming, normal people like you and me were ushered into the realm of the supernatural. Then, when Jesus actually made His first appearance, more angels appeared, tumbling over the edges of heaven, filling the sky with an other-worldly proclamation, and generally scaring the wits out of some unsuspecting sheep herders. Oh, and don't forget that star. It led some wise seekers on the journey of a lifetime and compelled them to bring an array of gifts that were costlier than anything Mary or Joseph would have imagined they'd ever see, let alone receive on behalf of their Child.

Some events call for extravagance.

I'm sure that today's scripture reading will prompt your memory of how the days surrounding the death, burial, and resurrection of Jesus were chock full of unbelievable, inexplicable occurrences. Earthquakes, a torn temple veil, and dead people walking—all this pointed to the fact that something really big was happening. (And you can file that thought with the Department of Understatements.)

Worship calls for extravagance. Each time we gather, we remember and in some ways reenact the death, burial, and resurrection of Jesus. Do you recall the lady mentioned in Mark 14 and in John 12? She presented an extravagant offering of devotion to her Lord, and Jesus not only received it, but also defended her actions.

Our extravagance in worship leads to an offering of all we are, to the only One worthy to receive it. It can be costly, and it can take some preparation. It can be inconvenient at times, and we might even be criticized for it. It's just worth it.

Some events call for extravagance.

*Lord Jesus, You are truly worthy of our deepest, most costly,
most extravagant worship. You went to the deepest, most costly,
most extravagant lengths for us. Amen*

- Do you ever feel that worship is costly? Inconvenient? Extravagant?
- Do you feel that it's worth it?

Notes...

39
Created For Praise

... the people I formed for myself
that they may proclaim my praise.
(Isaiah 43:21)

Do you ever wonder why you're here? What your purpose is? Why you were created? If so, you're not alone. Most of us have wondered at times if we're on the right track and if we're fulfilling our potential. We train and we educate ourselves so that we can be all we're meant to be, and yet there's one ultimate calling that's common to all of us.

Isaiah's people knew about this conundrum. They were "God's chosen people," yet their history was marked by civil unrest and warring neighbors. They were promised a Prince of Peace, but what they got most was a predicament of persecution. To be honest, a lot of their troubles were the result of their own foolish choices and sinful decisions. We can be a lot like that, can't we?

Right in the middle of Isaiah's astounding prophecy comes a brilliant flash of optimism for a nation long enshrouded in darkness. God speaks: "Forget the former things; do not dwell on the past." Move on. Turn the corner. Let it go.

"See, I am doing a new thing! Now it springs up; do you not perceive it?" God has always been in the business of restoration, of fresh hope, of second chances. He works out the impossible. He makes crooked paths straight. He mends the broken, and He revives the sick. But it's all for a purpose: that God's people, whom He formed for Himself, would declare His praise.

Jesus said that if we don't praise Him, the very rocks will cry out (see Luke 19:40). So, do you ever wonder why you're here? What your purpose is? Why you were created?

You were created for praise.

Lord, we see that even in our brokenness, You have never removed
the calling on our lives. We long to live out what we were created
for—to proclaim Your praise. Amen

- How have you felt God's touch of restoration and healing?
- How can that be turned into praise?

Notes...

40
God Thoughts

The LORD your God is with you, he is mighty to save.
He will take great delight in you, he will quiet you with
his love, he will rejoice over you with singing.
(Zephaniah 3:17)

When you think of God, what comes immediately to mind? An angry judge? A stern task-master? A vengeful deity? If these are your first thoughts, today's reading has good news for you!

While it's true that Zephaniah's prophecy was intended as a warning about Judah's approaching judgment, there are slivers of hope embedded here that, by extension, offer us hope and a more accurate view of the nature and character of our heavenly Father.

There are shades of our old friend Isaiah in verse 15 of Zephaniah 3. Isaiah recorded this message from God:

"Comfort, oh comfort my people," says your God. "Speak softly and tenderly to Jerusalem, but also make it very clear that she has served her sentence, that her sin is taken care of—forgiven! She's been punished enough and more than enough, and now it's over and done with." (Isaiah 40:1–2 MSG)

Has it ever crossed your mind that, despite your failures and despite your doubting, God is with you, mighty to save, and taking great delight in you? Sometimes that's hard to imagine, isn't it? We all know that context is key to understanding a scripture passage. Still, I think you'd agree that God's character never changes, and His Word is given to us to encourage us even today.

"He will quiet you with his love," wrote Zephaniah. Martin Luther paraphrased it like this: "He will cause you to be silent so that you may have in the secret places of your heart a very quiet peace and a peaceful silence." I like that.

Finally, Zephaniah writes, "He will rejoice over you with singing." Imagine it: God singing a joyful song over you and me. It may help to know that the original Hebrew word, translated here as "rejoice," indicates a *whirling dance!* Now, what comes to your mind when you think of God?

And just as importantly, how will you respond?

> *Father, just to think that You would take delight in me, You would sing over me, is almost more than I can comprehend. Thank You for Your love. Thank You for showing Yourself mighty to save. Amen*

- How does your worship reflect your view of God?
- Does anything need to be changed?

Notes...

41
Confession

If we confess our sins, he is faithful and just and will forgive us
our sins and purify us from all unrighteousness.
(1 John 1:9)

We don't hear as much about it these days. Even in our worship gatherings, we tend to downplay it. We love to celebrate, and we love reveling in the wonders of God. But often, something's missing, and in order to take on the full counsel of scripture, we have to consider it. More than just considering it, we have to adopt a cloak of humility and embrace it. It's called confession, and today's reading has a good bit to say about that.

We get the word "confess" by translating the Greek word *homologeo*, and it means "to say the same thing as." It indicates accepting God's view of our actions. All this is a reflection of the opening portion of Psalm 32, and especially verse 5 of that passage:

Then I acknowledged my sin to you and did not cover up my iniquity. I said, "I
will confess my transgressions to the LORD*"—and you forgave the guilt of my sin.*

One of the saddest realities in the world today is the belief that we have to get it all together before we can enter the doors of the Church. The underlying thought is "I've made such a mess of my life that God would never want me to come to Him. He could never love the likes of me." But friend, if we can't accept each other, support each other, and encourage each other while extending God's love as the Body of Christ, where in the world is that supposed to happen? I like what my wife, Vicki, says on this matter: The Church is a hospital for sinners, not a hotel for saints!

"Free us for joyful obedience," says the ancient liturgy. Here's the good news: we confess; He forgives. We're all in the same boat here.

And heaven help us if we ever forget.

Lord, we come sinful, broken, and hurting, confessing our sins
before You. Forgive us and free us for joyful obedience. Amen

- Does confession play a significant role in the worship gatherings of your church?
- How can you encourage those around you to come to God just as they are?

42
Carried On Everlasting Arms

✤ Deuteronomy 33:26–29 ✤

***The eternal God is your refuge, and
underneath are the everlasting arms.***
(Deuteronomy 33:27a)

Sometimes when we think about worship, we don't need to think about Church history or tradition. We don't need to think about modern adaptations or being "relevant." And we certainly don't need to think about what others are doing and what they might think of us. Sometimes when we think about worship, what we need to think about is our own personal history with God: what He's brought us through and where He's leading us today.

Sometimes we need to simply remember that *olam zerowa*, the everlasting arms, are beneath us and that the eternal God is our refuge. We need to remember, too, that David, Israel's most passionate worship leader, had these thoughts as well, and they're recorded in 2 Samuel 22:31: "He is a shield for all who take refuge in [God]."

David was, no doubt, familiar with Israel's history, and I'm pretty sure he would have been well aware of the song of Moses that we find in today's reading. Both David and Moses include the word "shield," and its imagery is perfect: a protector, a buckler, a defensive device. I find it fairly amusing, but again, perfectly appropriate, that the word for "shield" was also used to define the scaly hide of a crocodile! You wouldn't even want to get near that, but that's sort of the point, isn't it?

Sometimes when we think about worship, all we really need to do is look back and remember how God has been our shield and our protector, how He's been the everlasting arms that have carried us through difficult seasons, and how He's been our refuge in times of trouble.

And whatever you're facing right now, you can be assured of this: what He did before, He can do again.

*Lord, You are our dwelling place and our eternal refuge. Thank You
for the times You carried us in yesterday's troubles and for the promise
that You'll carry us in tomorrow's challenges. Amen*

- How have you seen God as a protective shield in your life?
- How have you responded to Him?

Notes...

43
A Covenant Relationship

Then he took the Book of the Covenant and read it to the
people. They responded, "We will do everything the Lord
has said; we will obey."
(Exodus 24:7)

It's so like God to take the normal, mundane, day-to-day aspects of our lives and, with His touch, sanctify them. Covenants are a great example of this. During the times that we read about in the Bible, covenants were more like commercial, political transactions or agreements. They generally included a *Suzerain,* the greater and more powerful entity, and a *Vassal,* the subservient entity. Covenants would employ language or concepts along the lines of: *You do this for me, and I'll do that for you. You provide protection and land for us, and we'll supply service and allegiance to you. You be our king, and we'll be your people.*

A Suzerain/Vassal covenant would have been ratified and stored in the shrine of the deity sworn by. The ratification process included some sort of animal sacrifice, indicating "May [deity sworn by] do this to us if we fail to uphold the agreement in this covenant." It was pretty common stuff, but it was also pretty important stuff.

When God began speaking to His people in covenant terms, they would have understood the concept: Yahweh would be their Suzerain, their Protector King, and they would be His Vassal, His loyal servants. The well-known covenant with Abraham in Genesis 15 depicts how such an agreement, so familiar to wealthy businessman landowner Abraham, could be made sanctified, holy.

Now, fast-forward a few thousand years to when Jesus has gathered with His disciples to share the Passover meal during which, according to the ritual, God's covenant with Israel was always recounted. Jesus reinterprets the covenant language (see Matthew 26:27 and Luke 22:20) and says, "This cup is the *new* covenant in *my* blood..." Recalling the words of Exodus 20, Jesus is saying, "*I* am your Suzerain; *I* will deliver you from the bondage of sin; *I* will be your protector." And with the drinking of the cup, the covenant is ratified.*

In response to the new covenant in which we are now partakers, our worship should move us to action. To be His people. To serve Him. The covenant sacrifice has once and for all been paid.

Lord Jesus, how we praise You as both our Protector and our
sacrificed Lamb. We are Your people, and You are our God. Amen

- Have you considered your relationship to Jesus a covenant?
- How does this covenant relationship move you to worship?

Notes...

44
Overcoming Distractions

* Ephesians 6:10–18 *

For our struggle is not against flesh and blood, but against the rulers,
against the authorities, against the powers of this dark world
and against the spiritual forces of evil in the heavenly realms.
(Ephesians 6:12)

Do you ever feel distracted as you enter a time of worship? I know I do. *Is the choir prepared? Are the instrumentalists going to get that modulation? Does the temperature in the sanctuary feel right? Why didn't anyone replace that lightbulb? Why is the soloist always late for sound checks? And where is so and so? They didn't tell me they'd be missing today!*

Sound familiar? You probably have a list of frequent distractions that you could add to this. I don't know if you've ever considered this, but distractions can be a subtly effective tactic employed by the enemy of your soul to divert your attention away from God. You see, our adversary despises our worship, and he's not above any assault that will keep us from voicing our praise. Our battle isn't really against all the distractions that hit us on a Sunday morning. Our struggle is with unseen forces that cower at the name of Jesus.

Paul mentions "the devil's schemes" in today's scripture reading. *Methodeia* is the Greek word he used, and you can easily see how we get our word "method." In this case, it's best defined as "wiles, strategies, trickery, craftiness, or deceit." And what an accurate description this is! How often these schemes have manifested themselves in the trap of comparisons, or in feelings of inadequacy and inability, or in the deception of unworthiness resulting in a severe lack of confidence.

All these are distractions, my friend, that can be overcome by standing strong and voicing the glories of Him who has overcome even the unseen forces that wage war against us. You see, praise erases distractions and chases away the enemy—even when the altos miss that cut-off.

Lord, we see how petty distractions can shift our focus away from You. Give us
eyes to see beyond the schemes of our enemy and into the eyes of our Savior. Amen

- Have you ever thought of worship as spiritual warfare?
- How can you overcome the distractions that hinder your praise of God?

45
Worship in Sorrow

Then I heard a voice from heaven say, "Write: Blessed are
the dead who die in the Lord from now on."
(Revelation 14:13a)

The world is watching us. They're watching to see how we'll react to a crisis, how we'll respond to a tragedy. They're watching to see if what we boldly profess when the sun is shining will be the same song we sing when darkness envelops us.

Nowhere is our faith tested to any greater extent than in the face of death. Death can be sudden. Death can be cruel. Death dashes hopes and crushes dreams. It's the final enemy according to 1 Corinthians 15:26, and so many times, it does seem to stamp "finality" on everything it touches.

Brothers, we do not want you to be ignorant about those who fall asleep,
or to grieve like the rest of men, who have no hope. (1 Thessalonians 4:13)

There it is: Hope. It's not hope in the sense of wishful thinking, but hope in the sense of assured expectation. It's hope as in the affirmation of those things we know to be true.

Though the fig tree does not bud and there are no grapes on the vines, though the
olive crop fails and the fields produce no food, though there are no sheep in the
pen and no cattle in the stalls, yet I will rejoice in the LORD, I will be joyful in
God my Savior. (Habakkuk 3:17–18)

Can you say the same thing? When the job is terminated and income runs thin before it runs out? When disagreements fester and the relationship is broken? When disease runs rampant and death appears to have the final say?

Look back at verse 3 in today's reading from Revelation 14. That "new song" mentioned there implies *quality* as opposed to *chronology*. It was a "new" song because it had an entirely different quality from anything they'd sung before. It was birthed of a

94

special, unique experience—an experience leading to hope, promise, and victory. The song of the overcomer.

The world is watching, and the world is listening for the song we'll sing.

> *Father, this day we choose to praise You. In the midst of struggle, in the midst of strife, in the midst of defeat, we choose to praise You. Amen*

- How do catastrophes, disasters, and disappointments color the way you worship?
- What kind of example can you set when tragedy strikes?

Notes...

46
Your Act of Worship

✦ Romans 11:30–31; 12:1–2 ✦

Therefore, I urge you, brothers, in view of God's mercy,
to offer your bodies as living sacrifices, holy and pleasing
to God—this is your spiritual act of worship.
(Romans 12:1)

Every word we see rendered as "worship" in our English Bibles has, in its original language, a physical gesture implied by it. The Hebrew word *shachad* is used 81 times in the Old Testament, and it means "to bow, bend low, or prostrate oneself." *Yadah* indicates "to address God with extended hands." We see the Greek word *proskuneo* mentioned 51 times in the New Testament, and one of its definitions is "to kiss toward," implying a sense of intimacy.

Latreia is the word Paul used in today's key verse, where we read "this is your spiritual act of worship." *Latreia* means "worship, or service, or worship through service." It's active, not passive. It's involved, not detached. It's invested participation, not a spectator sport.

Latreia is a response to the mercy of God. By responding to God's mercy, we offer ourselves, and we allow ourselves to be transformed by the renewing of our minds. Transformation (*metamorphous*) is a change that occurs from the inside out. The results may have an outward, visible manifestation, but the cause is an inward change. *Latreia* means we find our place in the Body of Christ. We discover our position for the greatest influence and contribution. We search out our potential for lasting impact.

A "living sacrifice" seems oxymoronic. Everybody knows that to sacrifice something you have to kill it. In sacrificing our will, our desires, and even our way of thinking, we die to ourselves only to find life in Christ.

A living sacrifice plus a renewed mind equals a spiritual act of worship.

Lord Jesus, we surrender to the transformation that can only
come from You. Renew our minds as we present ourselves today
as living sacrifices. Amen

- What are you willing to sacrifice in order to gain a renewed mind?
- How does your spiritual act of worship manifest itself?

Notes...

47
Wounded

◈ Genesis 32:22–31; 33:1–11 ◈

The sun rose above him as he passed Peniel,
and he was limping because of his hip.
(Genesis 32:31)

Jacob knew a lot about wounds. He'd been wounded in a wrestling match with a man whom many scholars believe was God Himself disguised as an angel. He had wounded relationships with his brother Esau and with his father-in-law Laban that took years to mend. He was even wounded at birth—the name his parents gave him means "supplanter." That'll leave an emotional scar! Oh, and he had two wives. I'll leave it at that.

Today's scripture reading is a bit lengthy, but it's important in order to get a snapshot of this portion of Jacob's life. If you read the full account of him in Genesis 25–35, you'll see right away that he moved around a lot, and in those moves, he received some wounds, a few of which were self-inflicted. Still, you have to admire the fact that Jacob maintained a certain passion for God and regularly took the time and made the effort to recognize the hand of God in his life. As a result, God kept His promise of blessing and changed Jacob's name to Israel. He was renamed and thus redefined.

We can learn and apply a few things from Jacob's story that have a direct impact on how we relate to each other and how we respond to God in worship.

Wounded leaders often know best how to minister to others who are, or who have been, wounded. Experience is a great teacher, and lessons learned can be passed on to those who are not only hurting, but receptive in their spirit as well. Scars are a sign of healing, and the Body of Christ should demonstrate an eager willingness to invest in the healing process.

Speaking of which, it's been said (sadly) that the Church is the only army that shoots its wounded. Those who, like Jacob, walk with a limp, may in fact know more of the mercy and grace of God than those who are "perfectly healthy" ever will. Let's not be so quick with our judgment.

Sometimes, God wounds us to make us walk differently, distinctly. His transforming encounters are often wrestling matches, and He will on occasion injure us to get us to submit to the blessing. In every struggle, like Jacob, do not let go until the blessing comes, and you are renamed, redefined.

O God, as we minister to those around us who are wounded,
wound us, also, if it brings us Your blessing. Amen

- What wounds do you carry with you?
- Are you willing to share those for the sake of others?

Notes...

48
A Word about the Word

In the beginning was the Word,
and the Word was with God,
and the Word was God.
(John 1:1)

If you're a Word Nerd like me, then etymology is a fascinating area of study for you. Words equal ideas, and ideas have consequences.

Biblical Greek language uses primarily two terms for what we see translated as "word": *Rhema* and *Logos*. Some scholars will tell you that *Rhema* designates a spoken, expressly stated, "right now" word or portion of scripture that can be applied to our daily lives for this moment's particular situation. They'd say that *Logos* refers to the total inspired Word of God, His full and divine expression, His revelation to us.

Other equally God-fearing scholars would tell you that there's no difference at all in the two words. They'd say that it's a matter of style or, at most, a subtle and nuanced difference. In their opinion, we could use the words interchangeably.

In these opening verses of John's gospel in today's reading, Jesus is referred to as the Word. John chose *Logos* to describe Jesus here, and the really important thing to glean from this is that "the Word (*Logos*) was God." Actually, the Greek phrasing is "Theos en ha Logos"—literally, "God was the Word."

There are those who would try to convince you that Jesus never claimed deity, or that at most, He is *a* god. We might be tempted to fall for that if we didn't have Jesus' own words (*Rhema?*) about Himself scattered throughout the New Testament. He was, and is, all He ever claimed to be, or else He was a raving lunatic!

It all comes down to "Who is Jesus?" We have the testimony—the full, divine, authoritative word of scripture—to guide us and to assure us that when we worship Jesus, we're worshiping God.

Jesus, You are the Word, spoken by the Father and revealed to us in
the scriptures. Your word is truth, and that truth has set us free. Amen

- Can you articulate and defend your belief that Jesus is God?
- Does your worship reflect this?

49
In It Together

❖ Numbers 12:1–9 ❖

"Has the Lord spoken only through Moses?" they asked.
"Hasn't he also spoken through us?" And the Lord heard this.
(Numbers 12:2)

Today's scripture reading portrays a story we don't hear very much about. That may be because it's not a particularly pretty story. Most aren't when they're centered on comparison and its cousins, jealousy and envy. Nothing tears down a relationship like these three, and nothing will destroy a ministry in the way these hideous culprits can.

You can see it for yourself—Moses' brother and sister start to feel a little left out, a little ignored, and a lot hurt. "What about us? Aren't we as good?" is the underlying theme of their complaint. If you step back and read Numbers 11:26–30, you'll see that even Joshua was prone to allowing a protective spirit to pervade. He encouraged Moses to, for his own sake, be territorial and closely guard the prophetic gift that had been entrusted to him, as if this sort of thing had exclusivity attached to it.

Moses' response is golden: "I wish that all the Lord's people were prophets and that the Lord would put his Spirit on them!"

Ministry is not the property of ministers. Any gifting we receive is not for our own benefit, and especially not for our own elevation. Now, it's always a good and healthy thing to be aware of what God is doing in other congregations and among other people, but comparisons between other leaders, ministries, or churches should have no place among us. God works how and where He will with whom He will. There is no competition between lighthouses.

We're in this together, you know. When one segment of the Body of Christ is broken, we all should feel the fracture. When your church hurts, my church hurts. And when you rejoice, I can rejoice!

There's a big world out there that doesn't care much about our internal comparisons or our petty jealousies. For their sake, and for the sake of the gospel, let's remember that we're in this together.

*Lord Jesus, remind us of our unity that comes through Your Spirit.
Remove our petty jealousies and our worthless comparisons.
We ask this for the sake of Your gospel. Amen*

- Have you been tempted to compare your ministry with that of anyone else?
- How do you overcome any feelings of envy or jealousy?

Notes...

50
Gifts and Freedom

❀ 1 Corinthians 14:26–28, 14:36–40 ❀

But everything should be done in a fitting and orderly way.
(1 Corinthians 14:40)

If you'd like to start a good, old-fashioned heated debate, then initiate a discussion on speaking in tongues among believers of differing persuasions. Nothing, unfortunately, seems to be more divisive in the Church today. Heads-up: we're not going to do that here!

But speaking in tongues *is* mentioned in today's reading. That said, a defense of or opposition to it isn't really the point. What Paul seems to be advocating is a certain deference, courtesy, and respect for other believers. And that's a good word to us, as well.

Above all, Paul is saying that when we gather for worship, things should be done "in a fitting and orderly way." Or, as some translations (like the King James Version) word it, "decently and in order." I suppose that what's fitting, orderly, and decent might be up for debate also, but it all has to do with honesty, with intent and motivation. We allow each other the freedom to hear from God, to respond to God, and to exercise our spiritual gifts without fear of suppression. Likewise, if our responses cause confusion or discomfort among the body of believers, we'd best keep them private.

By the way, "decently and in order" doesn't mean "stodgy and predictable." It doesn't mean that things are set in stone with no room for spontaneity. It doesn't mean that proper preparation (which is a good thing!) always takes precedence over an immediate word from God. On the other hand, God can speak to us six months out just as clearly as He can five minutes before a worship service is to begin.

Gifts are meant for giving, and giving is meant for receiving. How beautiful when a gift, given and received, is perfectly appropriate.

Lord, Your gifts to Your Church are amazing! Give us the grace to
receive them and to share them in a way that builds up the
fellowship of believers. Amen

- Is there room for freedom of expression in your congregation?
- How respectful are you of the gifts of others?

Notes...

51
Another Word on Freedom
(From and For)

❖ Galatians 5:1, 5:13–15 ❖

It is for freedom that Christ has set us free.
(Galatians 5:1a)

Here's another word on freedom. This time, we're not looking at freedom in worship like we did when we read from 1 Corinthians 14. Here, we're talking about personal freedom in our everyday lives and how that freedom interacts with those around us, those to whom and with whom we minister. Let's dig in.

It helps to remember that the friends in Galatia who Paul was writing to were, of course, recent converts. Christianity was in its infancy, and the Church was just getting off the ground. Somehow, the Galatians' belief system had been infused with the fallacy that they must adhere to "the law" despite their faith in Christ. This, naturally, caused quite a doctrinal dilemma, and so Paul sets out to explain to them that Christ's calling on them includes freedom _from_ and freedom _for_.

They were free _from_ sin and death. They were free _from_ self-sufficiency. They were free _from_ misperceptions and false teaching. They were free _from_ self-centeredness.

Likewise, they were free _for_ service. They were free _for_ loving others. They were free _for_ recognizing that it's not about what they did, but about what Christ has done.

So, what does all that mean to us? It means we can and should use our freedom to serve others. It means we can and should exercise our gifts not for our own glory or benefit, but for the good of the entire Body of Christ. It means we can and should love our neighbor as ourselves.

It means freedom _from_ and freedom _for_ are two sides of the wonderful gift we call grace.

_Lord Jesus, Your grace has freed us from the law and freed us for
serving others. We celebrate this gift, and we worship You, the Giver. Amen_

- How well do you serve others in your particular area of ministry?
- Do you use your gift for the benefit of the entire Body of Christ?

52
The Convenient Route

*So David went down and brought up the ark of God from
the house of Obed-Edom to the City of David with rejoicing.*
(2 Samuel 6:12b)

The tale is a little troubling to say the least. David has regained possession of the Ark of the Covenant, which had been captured by his warring neighbors, the Philistines. As they're returning it to Jerusalem, one of the oxen pulling the cart that was carrying it stumbles. Well-intentioned Uzzah reaches out to steady the Ark so it won't fall, and God strikes him dead. Does this bother you just a little bit?

Except, God had already told them how to carry or transport the Ark, how to handle the "holy things" (see Exodus 25:10–16 and Numbers 4:5, 4:15). What the Israelites were doing in today's story was simply replicating the way they'd seen the Philistines carry it off previously. And that's where the disaster began.

We can learn a few things from this saga, not the least of which is that while God allows us great freedom in how we respond to Him, He does have certain expectations about the attitude with which we approach Him. When we take the expedient, convenient route in worship, rather than considering God's directives and expectations, we're in trouble.

The Israelites did it the way the Philistines had done it. In establishing His new kingdom, God wanted His children to be different from the world around them. His kingdom was to be established on His Word. There's a distinct, authentic, and authenticated relationship between reverence and blessing.

I have a theory that I'm not sure I can prove, but I believe it to be true: *most people will never go deeper in their worship experience than those who are leading them.* Those of us who are "upfront" in worship are to handle the "holy things" of God as both an example and as an encouragement.

*Father, we are so grateful for the freedom You allow us in responding
to You. Help us to see clearly and to honor Your expectations of us. Amen*

- What expectations do you sense God has for approaching Him?
- Have you ever been guilty of taking the expedient, convenient route?

Notes...

53
God's Halfway Point

⁂ Exodus 25:1–9 ⁂

"Then have them make a sanctuary for me,
and I will dwell among them."
(Exodus 25:8)

Much has been said and written about the Old Testament tabernacle with its intricate design, its elaborate furnishings, and its deep significance. It did, after all, house that inner sanctum, the Most Holy Place or the Holy of Holies, where God said He would meet with His people. Beyond merely representing the presence of God, it housed the presence of God.

You can easily see why the directives for the construction and transporting of this mobile house of worship would be so vitally important to Moses and his wandering congregation. Israel was a sojourning nation, and their travels led them to interact with other nations that, if they had gods at all, worshiped deities that were man-made and plentiful, yet far off and distant. The tabernacle was a tangible, visible reminder that the one true God had deigned to dwell with His people.

But the tabernacle was only the "halfway point" in God's journey. His deepest desire was and still is to dwell *in* us. John's gospel declares that the Word—God incarnate— became flesh and blood and made His dwelling among us (John 1:14). The Amplified Bible puts it this way: "And the Word became flesh and *tabernacled* (fixed His tent of flesh, lived awhile) among us." Not secluded, not isolated, not at arm's length. But actually walking around, eating, drinking, and sleeping among us.

There's one more step in God's journey to be with His beloved. That's the step to be *in* us. That's why Jesus promised that once He had left this earth, He'd send a Counselor, a Comforter, the Holy Spirit to guide us, to lead us, to dwell in us (see John 14:16, 14:26, 16:13 and Ephesians 1:13–14).

Only God's unfathomable love would lead Him to take the unthinkable step of being with us so that we would have the unimaginable joy of having Him in us.

*O God, Your desire to dwell not only with us, but in us leaves us amazed and
grateful. We honor You as the God who became one of us so that we might
be with You forever. Amen*

- How does your worship reflect the realization that God is not only among us, but within us?
- How would worship in your congregation be different if everyone had this realization?

Notes...

54
Small Things and God's Spirit

❖ Zechariah 4:1–10 ❖

"Not by might nor by power, but by my Spirit," says the LORD Almighty.
(Zechariah 4:6b)

God often chooses to do extraordinary things through the hands of ordinary people—people like you and me, and Zechariah and Zerubbabel.

You're not familiar with Zerubbabel? He was appointed by Cyrus of Persia to be governor of Judah when some of the Jewish exiles were allowed to return to their homeland. One of their main tasks was rebuilding the temple in Jerusalem, and it was a pretty big task at that. Israel had been conquered, humiliated, and dragged off to a strange land. Capturing your enemy and bringing them home with you was a customary tactic of war in those days, a status symbol that brought a degree of prestige and a whole lot of ego boosting.

So Zerubbabel and his compatriots return, and the first question is "where to start?" Rebuilding the temple was going to be a huge undertaking, a huge responsibility, and probably a huge headache. Yet, the process of reconstructing the house of God was a first step in re-establishing the kingdom of God's people. A bit overwhelmed, Zerubbabel receives, through the prophet Zechariah, this word from the Lord: "Not by might nor by power, but by my Spirit."

I'm guessing that at some point you've felt overwhelmed in some aspect of your ministry role. The task before you is enormous, and you don't really even know where to start. Am I speaking to anyone? Zerubbabel would tell you this: *start small, one increment at a time. Take the next logical step or make the next logical decision. And don't rely on your own might, power, skill, or knack, but rely on God's Spirit.*

You can't, but He never said you could.

He can, and He always said He would.

Father, by Your Spirit we know that all things are possible. Give us eyes to see and hearts to receive all that You would say. Amen

- Are you facing what seems to be an insurmountable task today?
- What will you rely on to accomplish it?

Notes...

55
Eagerly Desiring

And he said to them, "I have eagerly desired to
eat this Passover with you before I suffer."
(Luke 22:15)

It may have escaped your notice when you've read this passage before. Jesus "eagerly desired" to share this Passover meal with His beloved. Why this particular Passover? Certainly, He was painfully aware that this would be His last with them here on earth. But beyond that, I tend to think that Jesus had so much to share with them and so little time. The Passover meal would be the perfect backdrop to help them see the perfect Passover Lamb, soon to be broken and poured out for them, for the whole world, for all time. And so, He eagerly desired to share with them.

Jesus would have led them in the *Kiddish*, the prayer of sanctification over the four cups of wine, commemorating the four "I wills" of Exodus 6:6–7, now infused with new life and new meaning. As recorded in Exodus, God speaks to Moses:

> *Therefore, say to the Israelites: "I am the* Lord*, and I will bring you out from under the yoke of the Egyptians. I will free you from being slaves to them, and I will redeem you with an outstretched arm and with mighty acts of judgment. I will take you as my own people, and I will be your God. Then you will know that I am the* Lord *your God, who brought you out from under the yoke of the Egyptians."*

Jesus speaks of *His* body being broken for them, *His* blood poured out for them, and a *new* covenant. He's adapting the ancient liturgy and saying, "*I* am your Lord. *I* will bring you out from under the yoke of sin, and *I* will free you from it. *I* will redeem you and take you as My own."

And so, He eagerly desires to share this with them … and with us. *Remember,* He says. *Remember this the next time you eat the bread and drink the cup.*

Lord Jesus, we thank You for your sacrifice to redeem
and rescue us. We will remember. Amen

- Does Communion (or The Lord's Supper or The Eucharist) ever feel routine or compulsory to you?
- What steps can be taken to breathe new life into this?

Notes...

56
Rooted and Established in Love

❖ Ephesians 3:14–19 ❖

And I pray that you, being rooted and established in love,
may have power, together with all the saints, to grasp how
wide and long and high and deep is the love of Christ.
(Ephesians 3:17b–18)

When you pray for your worship team, what do you pray for? Or, if you're a congregation member not involved in worship leadership, how do you pray for those who lead you? For their health and their strength? That their skills and abilities would increase for God's glory? That their insight into the Word would deepen and spill over into all they do?

If that's the way you pray for your worship team, please don't stop! These are essential needs for all those entrusted with leading God's people in worship. It's notable that Paul refers to these things in today's scripture passage about his prayer model for his friends in Ephesus, and he prays that they might be obtained "out of" (or "according to") God's glorious riches. We know that's an endlessly deep well to draw from, so it's a right and fitting way for Paul to pray.

But Paul goes beyond that and prays for their very foundation: that they be rooted and established in love; and that love become their first language, their first thought, their first response. Reflecting the love of Christ, this kind of love is (1) broad enough to include and reconcile everyone, always; (2) as long as eternity, with infinity as its stopping point; (3) deeper than the devastation of heartbreak or of sin; and (4) higher than all we could hope or imagine.

The worship team you lead, participate in, or pray for from the pew longs to feel appreciated, to feel cherished, and to feel accepted. We all do, don't we? Pray, first of all, that out of God's glorious riches, they'll be rooted and established in love for each other, for the Church, and for Christ.

Jesus, Your love is higher, longer, wider, and deeper than anything we
could ever imagine or conceive. Help us to reflect that love to one another. Amen

116

- How do you pray for your worship team?
- Will you begin now to pray that their first language, their first thought, their first response will be love?

Notes…

57
The Perfect Wedding

Then the angel said to me, "Write: 'Blessed are those who are invited to the wedding supper of the Lamb!'" And he added, "These are the true words of God."
(Revelation 19:9)

Weddings are joyful events for the most part. I say, "for the most part," because, let's face it, they can be daunting as well. There are so many decisions: the perfect date, the ideal location, what music to incorporate, who to involve, who to invite…

And because weddings are serious things, too, the Bible alludes to them in several passages. Jesus likens Himself to a bridegroom in Mark 2:18–20. Paul provides a beautiful analogy of marriage and the Church in Ephesians 5:22–30. And you remember the occasion that prompted Jesus' first recorded public miracle, don't you? (See John 2:1–11.)

Near the end of the book of Revelation (see today's reading), we witness a wedding. The timing is perfect, the location ideal. The music that's incorporated is profound. Those involved include twenty-four elders, four living creatures, and a great multitude in heaven. The celebration is great, and the sound of it all pierces the universe.

And those who are invited? Well, those guests are actually not guests at all. They are the Bride! The Bride of Christ. Christ who is the Groom; the One who loved His Bride and gave Himself for her.

"Let us rejoice and be glad and give him glory!" That's what verse 7 implores, and that's to be the attitude at this wedding. The Greek word for "be glad" is *agalliao*, meaning "to exult, to rejoice with exuberance, or *very much to leap.*" It's the same word used to describe Jesus Himself in Luke 10:21, and its Hebrew equivalent is found in Isaiah 61:10. This is no somber ceremony. It's a celebration of cosmic proportions.

And why not? Marriages are meant to be forever—'til death do we part. Here's a wedding that's for eternity. Death is no more, and the Bride is joined to her Groom never to part.

So rejoice and be glad! And if you're of a mind to, you're allowed *very much to leap!*

- How can this ultimate wedding mentioned in Revelation 19 affect our worship today in the here and now?
- How does tomorrow's anticipation inform today's celebration?

Notes...

58
Your God is Consistent

* Revelation 21:1–7 *

He who was seated on the throne said,
"I am making everything new!"
(Revelation 21:5a)

God is consistent, right? Do I really need to say that? Still, if you're like me, you'll come across some truth or insight from scripture that seems to portray God in a new way, a different way, almost as if He's acting out of character. Then, if you're like me, you'll realize that this is the way God's always been!

God has always (I mean, *always*) desired to be with us. He walked among Adam and Eve in the garden. He manifested His presence in the desert tabernacle and later in Jerusalem's temple. He took the unthinkable step of trading riches for rags, of exchanging glory for humility, of leaving splendor to inhabit squalor. He has always desired to be with us.

And God has always (I mean, *always*) been in the restoration business. He redeems and He restores so that we can return. Today's reading from Revelation 21 showcases the pinnacle of both concepts. "Now the dwelling place of God is with men, and he will live with them" (verse 3). That's forever and that's for always. It's the ultimate fulfillment of Exodus 25 and John 1. "To him who is thirsty I will give to drink without cost from the spring of the water of life" (verse 6). That's the embodiment of Isaiah 55 and John 4.

I'll say it again: God is consistent. "He who was seated on the throne said, 'I am making everything new!'" "Everything new" doesn't necessarily mean "all new things." God has always been in the restoration business. The end of one thing is the beginning of another. Go back and read Isaiah 40, and you'll be reminded that God has always made new ways; He's always done new things. Again, He restores and redeems so that we can return.

I have a feeling that may be good news for you today. It may be you that needs the promise of restoration or the touch of redemption. Be grateful, friend. Your God is consistent.

O God, thank You for always being a Redeemer and a Restorer.
Great is Your faithfulness to us. Amen

- How is restoration and redemption celebrated in your worship?
- Is it clearly presented for those who desperately need restoration and redemption?

Notes...

59
A Safe Place of Confidence

❖ Hebrews 4:9–16 ❖

Let us then approach the throne of grace with confidence, so that
we may receive mercy and find grace to help us in our time of need.
(Hebrews 4:16)

What would happen if next Sunday, as people entered your place of worship, everyone expected to walk right up to God? What if they really anticipated meeting Him face to face? How would that affect the way they prepared? How would that affect the way *you* prepared?

We're encouraged in today's key verse to approach God's throne of grace with confidence and with courage, not because of any merit of our own, but because God's throne of grace is a safe place. The One who dispenses grace can sympathize with us. He's been through it all, yet without sin. He's not a stand-offish kind of God. He's a warm and inviting God, and He's invited you and me.

So, why do we act as if He's distant, not hearing and not caring? Why are we hesitant to lay before Him our truest, deepest needs? James 4:2 tells us we don't have because we don't ask. James also says that when we ask, we should do so in faith, believing and not doubting. I'm afraid that we often ask in a timid, fearful way with a human-centered perspective. "Set your minds on things above, not on earthly things" (Colossians 3:2). "Devote yourselves to prayer, being watchful and thankful" (Colossians 4:2). That's boldness! That's confidence!

Look at it this way: the best advice is given to us by someone who understands our problem. The greatest help is offered to us by someone who has been through it and has overcome it.

In Jesus, we have both of these. Best of all, He's invited us to come to Him.

O Jesus, just now we accept Your invitation to come boldly to
Your throne. Thank You for the assurance that You hear,
You care, and You understand. Amen

- Does worship in your congregation reflect an actual access to God's throne?
- How would things change if everyone understood this?

Notes...

60
A Presence to Go with Us

❧ Exodus 33:12–15 ❧

***Then Moses said to [God], "If your Presence does not go
with us, do not send us up from here."***
(Exodus 33:15)

Finally! We're here! We've reached the end of our study of some of the most foundational scripture passages for us as worshipers. I hope you've been encouraged and
that maybe you've seen something in God's Word that you never saw before. I'm so
grateful to have been on this journey with you. Here's one last thought to leave with you.

We speak of it and we sing of it. We even pray for it. But do we really want it? Are we
really prepared for it?

The "it" here is God's presence. We speak of it, sing of it, and pray for it, oftentimes
forgetting that God's presence in our lives and in our worship can be an earth-shaking,
bone-rattling, life-altering epic occurrence. And if we can believe the biblical record at
all, it often comes with the assignment of some impossible-sounding task.

Ask Abraham, whose "flaming pot" episode challenged him to leave the familiar
place he loved and embark on a mystical journey with no clear destination. Ask Moses
at the burning bush, charged with leading a few million Hebrews out of bondage and
into a forty-year excursion.

Ask Joshua, whose lack of self-esteem caused God to continually implore him with
the command that he be strong and courageous. Ask Isaiah, whose vision of a thrice-
holy God included a rumbling temple, a poignant reminder of his own sinfulness, and
a commission to missionary service.

Or ask Job, whose flippant questioning of God resulted in him being shaken to the
core as God demanded that he stand like a man! Ask Mary, the mother of Jesus. And
ask Paul on his way to Damascus. They'll tell you. They'll explain to you how God's
showing up led them to a calling they never would have imagined or felt remotely prepared for.

True, God's presence can come to us warmly, in a whisper. But it can also come thun-
derously, as an all-consuming fire. And it always comes with a calling.

Are you ready for that?

124

- How have you experienced God's presence in your life and in your worship?
- What calling do you sense God has placed on you?

Notes...

128

757441